From Stage to Page
Annie Lisenby

Sir Ferdinand
Publishing

Sir Ferdinand Publishing

Contents

DEDICATION

This book is dedicated to all the storytellers, whether using literature, theatre, or other media.

Your stories help us understand our world and each other.

Never stop writing.

Introduction

Hello, readers, I'll make this short, because who actually loves a long introduction? I wrote this book after conversations with writer friends that led to speaking engagements at writing conferences and people asking for me to write down what I'd shared.

So, here it is.

This book is written from the source of my first true creative love, acting & theatre. I loved it so much that a bachelor's degree in theatre wasn't enough and I just had to go and earn a Master's of Fine Arts degree in acting and directing. I've acted on stages and taught in classrooms.

Like theatre, writing is storytelling. During the days when my children were young and staying up late at rehearsals wasn't an option, I flexed my creative muscles by writing my first stories. Quickly, I had a new creative love. All the lessons in this book are a mixture of lessons I taught in a classroom as a theatre teacher or chatted with an author friend over lunch at a writing conference.

This book is designed for writers to work through quickly and with activities to complete as you go. By the end, I hope that you have a richer grasp of your manuscript and are ready to get your words out into the world.

Thank you for spending your precious time with me through these pages.

Annie

PROLOGUE

Aristotle

WHAT DOES ARISTOTLE HAVE to do with theatre? Surprisingly more than people realize. During the Greek era, theatre was perfected to a form so well that the foundations developed during this time are still seen today across the Western world. During the Festival of Dionysus, there were theatrical competitions and awards given. Being that there were awards, there had to be a rubric for judging them. Enter Aristotle.

In his observations of these plays, Aristotle identified six elements of the drama: plot, character, thought (or theme), language (or diction), music, and spectacle. These elements were used to judge plays and in turn, to create plays with excellence. In this book, I'm going to take you through each of these elements of the drama and show you how lessons from theatre can help you add new life to your writing.

Chapter 1
PLOT

ARISTOTLE STATED THAT PLOT was the most important element of drama. Plot is the careful crafting of a dramatic (or literary) story. It's the difference between re-telling an event as it happened and carefully re-crafting the story so that it's shared with the intent of capturing an audience's attention. There are many craft books that break down plot in multiple ways. I'm going to discuss plot using something more simplified, something visual that I've used every time I've plotted a novel or short story.

Freytag's Pyramid. Gustav Freytag was a German theatre artist in the 1800's. His name doesn't come up too often in theatre circles unless they're talking about plot. Freytag broke down the building blocks of a plot into these elements: exposition, inciting incident, a series of crises, climax, denouement, and the resolution. Below is Annie's version of Freytag's Pyramid drawn out. It is often represented by a pyramid to demonstrate the building of tension toward the climax.

When looking at plot, it's important to answer or create all these elements for your manuscript. They don't have to be written into the story in great detail. Use what best works for your book. But know the foundations here to create the world and the plot so that you have a richly created story in your mind that will make your novel equally rich in details.

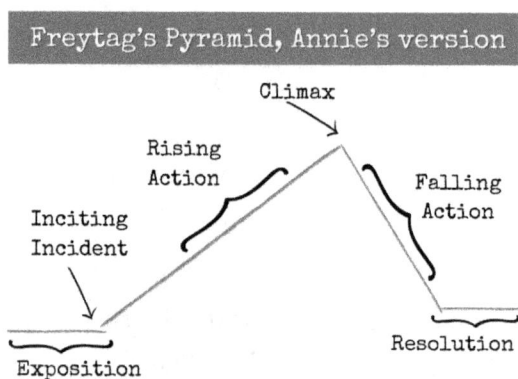

Freytag's Pyramid, Annie's version

Climax

Rising
Action

Falling
Action

Inciting
Incident

Resolution

Exposition

Exposition

Exposition is providing the necessary information needed for the audience (or reader) to enter and buy into the world of the play (or novel). I call these the "newspaper questions" because they're often taught when writing information pieces for a newspaper article.

Who? What? Where? When? Why?

When writing, you choose at what point to reveal these bits of information to your reader. Sometimes, the reader needs to know in the first chapter that they're being invited into a futuristic world full of cyborgs and a royal family so that they can invest in the story. Other times, an author will hold onto an important expository detail and reveal it at a pivotal point in the plot. How exciting is it to write a story where the reader learns that it's not actually 1950, but the time is 2250 on a new Earth where the inhabitants are trying to recreate the 1950s but failing miserably?

When determining the "who?" in a story, ask yourself, "Who is the main character?" This is determined by the character who changes most in the story. You could have multiple perspectives if you're writing a romance with dual points of view or a mystery with quadruple perspectives. But remember: each character will need their own arc, their own growth or journey to a new understanding through the course of the story. Chapter 2: Character will delve deeper into character arcs.

"What?" What is the character doing in the opening paragraph? This would be some kind of action. Are they playing baseball? Walking on the beach? Eating a cheeseburger? Determine what is happening at the start of the story.

"Where?" can be a deceivingly simple question. It's easy to write: John is playing baseball on the baseball field. And you might not need to provide more details to your reader. But if you can build a rich location in your mind it will help you share the world you're creating.

There can be a significant difference in the stories being told. For example, let's look at John. *John is playing baseball on the new Little League baseball field built by the new boss at the coal mine.* This tells one story.

John is playing baseball in the dusty yard surrounded by the ever-present tall fences topped with thick razor wire. Now, this story is totally different. John is still in a baseball field, but what a different field!

The "when?" of a story determines all the elements found in the story. Certainly, this applies to visual elements such as clothing styles, vehicles used, and technology available. But this also informs how the characters interact in their world. A student standing up in a college class to challenge their professor might not be shocking in 2023, but in 1923 it would have been unheard of. And if you have a story that time hops, you'll have even more fun filling in the varied details to delineate the different time periods.

"Why?" This is a more complex question that will be discussed more in Chapter 2: Character. For now, let's just ask ourselves, "Why is the character *where* they are, *when* they are, and doing *what* they are in the first chapters of the novel? And how does *who* the character is inform their interactions in that world?"

Specifics

Throughout this book, you will find me using the word "specifics" a lot. Like, really, a lot! In a play when a detail is repeated, this is because the playwright thought it was important. Same here. Specifics are important on stage and on the page. They add the extra layer of detail to pull your readers into the world you've created on the page.

Writing Rehearsal

Take a moment here to answer these questions about your current work in progress (WIP). Be as specific as possible because the more detailed, the more realistic the story will be. Use the questions below to build the exposition of your novel.

- **Who is(are) the main character(s)?**

- **What are they doing in the first paragraphs?**

- **Where is the action taking place?**

- **When does the story take place?**

- **Why is the character doing what they're doing in the first paragraphs?**

Inciting Incident

The inciting incident is the singular action that begins the conflict of the story. It's specific. It's not a war. It's a single bullet. It's not a packed college party. It's a pair of deep brown eyes that see into your soul.

I've had lively debates with students when evaluating a script or a film as to when the inciting incident happens. As an author, you need to know exactly when the inciting incident happens because it's the exact moment when the main character's life changes so that it will never be the same again. Depending on the genre of your book, this can look very different. One of my favorite inciting incidents from romance is found in Abby Jimenez's *The Friend Zone*. The female main character, Kristen, meets the male main character when she rear-ends him and discovers that he's the best man at Kristen's best friend's wedding.

From the theatre world, I would suggest that the inciting incident of Shakespeare's *Hamlet* is the exact moment Hamlet hears the ghost tell him that Hamlet's father was murdered. A writer friend of mine, Jessica Payne, writes thriller novels. In her debut, *Make Me Disappear* the main character makes the decision to stage her own kidnapping to escape her uber-controlling boyfriend. She'd thought of doing it before, but in that moment when she makes the call to set up her own kidnapping, that's when her life will never be the same again.

When the inciting incident occurs, a question is posed that will not be answered until the climax of the novel. In the theatre world, we call this the major dramatic question. Will Hamlet avenge his father's murder? Will she find a man who loves her even though she can't give him children? Will he survive sixth grade without being bullied? The major dramatic question isn't something you tell your readers, it's something they can infer easily from your story. A great example of this is when Katniss Everdeen "volunteers as tribute" in *The Hunger Games*. By this action, a question is posed about her survival and her ability to save her family (and even her district) from total ruin.

A Quick Note on Conflict

The conflict a character faces can be an internal conflict (battling addiction, overcoming anxiety, learning to love again, etc.) or an external conflict (an earthquake, a horde of zombies, that jackass trying to steal your job, etc.). Can a character face both kinds of conflict? Yes! Absolutely! Fear of failure in the face of a raging hurricane, that's both kinds of conflict. But as the author, you need to determine where the character's conflict is rooted and how they will overcome this challenge through the story.

Writing Rehearsal

Consider your current WIP and its inciting incident.

- **What is the inciting incident of your manuscript? Remember to make it specific!**

- **Based on the inciting incident, what question is posed that must be answered throughout the manuscript?**

A Series of crises

The series of crises can be seen as an obstacle course you are taking your character(s) through. Sometimes the character wins, sometimes they lose, but they must face challenges to reach their goals. Their challenges are directly related to the inciting incident and the major dramatic question.

A crisis looks different based on genre. In a romance, a crisis might be a blocked road that means the two love interests have to stay in a remote cabin on a cold and snowy night. In a mystery, a crisis might be the discovery of evidence that redirects the investigation.

When writing the series of crises, I usually identify at least five big challenges that I'm going to force my characters to face. I usually pepper in some smaller crises throughout too. In my mind, I think of an actual obstacle course. The character meets a proverbial wall. Do they go through it? Over it? Around it? Under it? Readers tend to enjoy stories where they see the characters win some and lose some. That's what keeps the pages turning, not knowing what will happen next. So, vary it. The character manages to scale the wall but barely makes it out alive when they dig under the next wall and encounter venomous snakes on the other side.

These crises should grow in intensity. Freytag used a pyramid shape to demonstrate this. The intensity of the conflict should rise with each challenge, growing more and more intense until something has to break. By identifying these crises in your story, you can create signposts to guide your writing. I often compare this to taking a hike. I know the pathway and where I want to go, but I need to look up occasionally and find the blaze markers to confirm I'm on the right path. By identifying your crises before you begin writing, you can help stay on the path. Or if you prefer to write your entire manuscript and then revise later, as you revise ask yourself if you've created enough challenges for the characters and built the conflict with each one.

When thinking about the characters winning and losing, also keep in mind the overall intensity of your character's challenges. If you take your readers on a journey where the conflict is so high through the entire book they might disengage because they need a break from the suspense. Instead, write in those breaks between the crises. I like using the example of a roller coaster. It's so much fun to scream as the coaster plunges, but riders need moments of the slow climb to the next drop to catch their breath. It also builds tension on the ride back up to a new peak making the rider question what's going to happen next. When you write your novel and are working from one crisis to the next, write in places for your reader to catch their breath and anticipate the next plunge. This is the reason Shakespeare wrote the gravedigger scene in *Hamlet*. It was at the beginning of the final act and gave the audience a break from the tension before he ramped it back up again.

Writing Rehearsal

Consider your current WIP and the crises you've written or planned to write.

- **What are the crises in your manuscript? Identify five of them.**

- **How does the conflict or tension for your main character(s) grow with each crisis?**

The climax

This is the highest point of conflict in a story. It's the point where something has to break. Like the inciting incident, this is one specific moment, not a whole scene. The choices made by the characters in this moment will answer the major dramatic question. Will she decide it's okay to love again? Will he seek ultimate revenge? Will they survive?

The climax is the part of your book where the reader is most fulfilled. Their heart is soaring with joy or their eyes are weeping in sorrow or they've found a new sense of understanding the world. These are big statements, yes. Your climax should be big. It's what you've been building toward since you first introduced the characters to your reader. The reader has been turning pages to see how the story ends, and this is your moment to shine as a writer.

For some authors, they may not know what the climax will be when they start writing. Some books can be written in this manner, but I always suggest throwing out ideas to keep you focused. In some genres, the reader expects a certain kind of climax. In romance, there should be a HEA (Happily Ever After) or readers of that genre might feel stilted. When writing a mystery series, the mystery must be solved (or at least partially solved leading to a sequel) for the reader to have a sense of completion.

Looking back at writing the crises that lead up to the climax, let me encourage you to go big. In the theatre world, we use the phrase "raise the stakes." This means that you as the author choose huge conflict for your characters. When the characters have bigger challenges to overcome, it's more interesting for the reader to watch them achieve or not achieve their goals. Keep in mind that the size of the conflict is determined through the eyes of the character. For some, walking down the street to buy a pack of gum at the convenience store is easy breezy, simple as pie. But for someone with severe anxiety, this task might feel impossible. I'll talk about character more in the next chapter where you'll learn ways to build rich, fully-formed characters full of strengths and weaknesses.

Part of the fun of writing a character is messing with them too. (I write this with a smirk.) Depending on genre and style, this can mean many different things. When I teach plot, I love using *The Hunger Games* as an example. Because of the films, my students were often familiar with the story line. In it, there are literal "game makers" who are messing with Katniss, the main character. If she goes too far from the action of the "game" they literally shoot fireballs at her to force her back into the action.

As an author, I love this illustration because that's how we use crises building to a climax to challenge our characters. Do they get too comfortable? Do something to shake up their world. Should it be a fireball? In a romance, probably not. But in an action or thriller, unleash those fireballs. And not just tiny fireballs, gigantic fireballs that nearly kill the main character and burn down the whole forest. That's raising the stakes. That's taking the conflict to a newer, more intense level that leads to a high-stakes climax.

Writing Rehearsal

Consider your WIP and the build up to the climax of your story.

- **You've already written your crises. After reading this section, especially about raising the stakes, do you still like them? If not, go back and adjust your crises. Make them more dramatic if you'd like.**

- **Once your crises are set, it's time to write the climax. What is the specific moment in your story that answers the major dramatic question, the moment that solves the challenges your main character has faced? Because it's specific, you should be able to write it in one or two sentences.**

Denouement and Resolution

The word "denouement" is French, translated as "unraveling." If you envision the conflict of your story as a rope or a spring that has been twisted over and over building the tension, at the climax that tension is released. This is the denouement. It's another moment for readers to catch their breath. What goes up must come down, hence Freytag using a pyramid illustration.

The tension has been built and the major dramatic question answered. So now what? The characters can have a moment to survey the effects of the climax. Did they win? Did they lose? The tension is unraveling and falling into a new world. The denouement doesn't need to last long, but it's a nice time to wrap up any loose ends. With subplots, this is a great place to reflect on those or bring them to completion too.

The denouement is the moment when everything that's been thrown up into the air comes back down. The resolution is acknowledging the new places where everything has landed. When Freytag indicated on his pyramid the exposition as a flat line, that was him identifying the stability of the world of the story before the conflict begins. The resolution is also a flat line. It's the new world created by the conflict, a new level of stability.

Remember that the inciting incident is an event or action that changes the character's world forever. Their life or lives will never be the same again. The resolution shows this new world as it is. It's a new exposition where the author can answer the same newspaper questions again. Some of these questions will have the same answer. For example, it might still be the same time period but only a few days later. Or it might be the same location. What's important is to identify what has changed in the character's world. What's more important is that you as the writer show the reader how the *character* has changed.

Are you writing a series? Here's the great thing about using Freytag's Pyramid: the resolution of book 1 can be the exposition of Book 2! If you've answered questions for the resolution of Book 1, then you have the foundation of the exposition for the sequel. And this goes on and on to the next book in the series.

Writing Rehearsal

Consider your WIP and what happens after the climax.

- **Denouement: How does the conflict in your story unravel or begin to relax immediately after the climax? Are there subplots or other plot threads that need to be tied up?**

- **Resolution: Go back and answer the newspaper questions about the new world of your story from the main character's perspective. Who? What? Where? When? Why?**

Structure

Freytag's Pyramid is helpful for many writers. It's a quick and simple aid to help writers as they pre-write and define the major plot points in their books. Use this in the way that works best for you. I'm a fan of writing this out on paper in a simplified format or using a display board and covering it in post-its that follow the outline of the pyramid.

This format of structuring plot has been used in theatre for over a hundred years. We use it to write a play or to analyze a play. You can try this out on your favorite book too. As you read, see if you can put the plot points into Freytag's Pyramid.

By using Freytag's Pyramid, you have the outline of a book. Hooray! Take a moment to celebrate. Now, take a deep breath because we need to talk some more about plot. Your plot is the points of your story that you are using to write your book.

When using Freytag's Pyramid, writers often create a chronological order to tell their story. That is, telling the story in the order in which it happened on a timeline. It follows a pattern of plot point A to plot point B to plot point C to plot point D and so on. It might look like this: A-B-C-D-E-F-G.

But there's always more than one way to structure a story. Some authors start at the end, and then go back to tell the whole story. That structure might look like this: G-A-B-C-D-E-F-G. And some stories beg to be told in more unconventional methods with chronology. They might look more like alphabet soup: G-A-D-A-B-C-A-F-A-E-G. Really, there's more than one way to tell your story. In the world of theatre, I always advised students that they could tell a story any way they wanted as long as they could maintain the audience's attention and not leave them confused. In theatre, there's often an intermission where confused audiences might leave the show in favor of ice cream over the second act.

I'd be remiss to write a book about theatre influences in writing without talking about act structures. In the modern theatre, a play is commonly presented in a two-act structure: act one, intermission, act two. It's a nice package that audiences today are comfortable with. Occasionally, modern plays will be written in a three-act structure. This is also the common model for film writing.

Generally, in act one, the exposition and inciting incident are introduced. Also, there might be the first crisis that is left as a cliffhanger to keep the audience wanting more. Act two covers the rest of the crises as the conflict and challenges grow. In act three, the final crisis leads to the climax, denouement, and resolution. This structure is common in film series too. This is why books or films often come in trilogies. The first book is essentially the first act of the overall story of the trilogy. For some authors writing a series, they will break down their individual book plots while keeping in mind the overarching plot of the entire series.

Writing Rehearsal

Consider your WIP and its plot structure and series potential.

- Think about your current work in progress. What would the story be if it was written chronologically (A-B-C-D-E-F-G)? Do you plan to keep it in this order? If not, what order to you plan to use?

- Are you working on a series? If so, what is the major conflict that will carry through all three (or more) books? How is this conflict addressed in each of the three books individually?

Chapter 2
CHARACTER

A QUICK TIP FROM ANNIE: *Don't write your novel like you're watching a movie. Write it like you're playing each character in the film.*

When I studied for my Masters of Fine Arts degree in Theatre Performance, my primary emphasis was in acting, creating characters on stage. I love creating characters, making them individual and rich with details. I've carried this love over to creating literary characters. And it's from an actor's perspective, I'm writing this section.

Creating a character from scratch using only our imagination and inspiration from the world around us can be a daunting task. There are so many layers and levels to people that it can be difficult to assemble them all. What you're going to discover next are ways to think about creating a character that will help you write well-formed, engaging characters. Is this an all-inclusive list? Not at all. If you have something more you like adding to your characters, do that too. This list is simply an outline with questions to answer that will help you develop your characters well before writing their stories.

Note

Use this for as many characters in your novel as you need. Maybe secondary or minor characters don't need as deep of a dive into the character development. But that choice is up to you, author friend.

The great thing about writing for literature is that the author can fully tell the complete story including the inner thoughts and feelings of characters... if they want to. When actors create a character, they look at two elements: *inner* and *outer*.

Outer Elements

The outer elements of a character are the things they see when they look in the mirror. When creating a character, I like to choose an image for my character and make notes about their physical specifics for continuity. Usually, I choose an image from the internet. Don't worry if it's copyrighted, this is just for your notes. I place the image in a document and include the notes about the character's outer aspects next to the image. In the first book I wrote, I accidentally changed a main character's eye color halfway through the book. Oops. Creating a written description for quick reference will help avoid this kind of error. I've also found that having this document with images of characters was helpful for my book cover designer when he was creating images of the characters for his design.

When writing about the outer appearance of a character, it's helpful to start with the simple descriptions you'd find on a driver's license: height, weight, and eye color. Other descriptions of colors can include skin tones, hair colors, and the presence of freckles or other skin colorations such as tattoos and scars.

Writing Rehearsal

- **Consider one of the characters in your work-in-progress. How would you describe them on a driver's license?**

- **Are they human, animal, magical creature, etc.?**

- **What is their gender?**

- **How tall or short are they?**

- **What are their hair and eye colors?**

Stature is the next element I consider. How does the character carry themselves? Imagine how a six-year-old child will skip across a lawn. Now, imagine how an octogenarian with a newly replaced hip would traverse the same lawn. The physicality of a character affects how they carry themselves.

For example, I've observed that taller people often slump their shoulders attempting to make themselves smaller. What about people who don't follow the expectations? My cousin is 6'8" and enters a room tall and proud as though he's ready to conquer the world. The way he carries himself versus another person of the same height will reveal something about each of their characters.

Lastly, with stature, consider how the character's stature will change depending on the circumstance. Some people will stand tall and defiant against their greatest foe, but they wilt when they are chastised by their mother or father.

Or does the character have an injury? A pet peeve of mine is when a character in a book, film, or play is injured, but the injury is quickly forgotten in the next scene. Yes, it's exciting to see a warrior battle a dragon and win even after they've been stabbed through the leg with the dragon's claw. But if that same warrior is dancing in victory ten minutes later, your readers are going to scoff at the lack of continuity. (Unless, you write fantasy. And even then, there better be a magical mosquito or an elf with healing powers who steps in before the dance begins.)

A character's style can say a lot about them. A quick description of what they're wearing can give your reader an image and understanding of the character. Just like people walking down the street today, characters on the page can use their style to express something about who they are and what they stand for. Sometimes, characters can dress in a way that goes against the grain or is considered inappropriate by the culture you've created.

Consider the stereotypes from a high school: football jock, cheerleader, nerd, theatre geek, teacher's pet. All of these give you a quick mental image of how they'd dress to express themselves or to fit into their clique. There will be more on clothing choices in the chapter on spectacle. For now, consider how your characters present themselves.

How does your character move through the world? This is something seen on the outside too. This is a great place to add a quirk or tick. As mentioned before, a child will move differently than an elderly person. Other considerations include injuries, deformities, disabilities, impairment, and training from sports or dance. For example, ballet dancers are known for walking with a turnout that makes their toes point to the sides.

In Shakespeare's *King Lear,* the title character is slowly losing his mind throughout the play. A challenge actors face is displaying this deterioration through the physicality of the character. Some actors choose to add a limp, others a tremoring hand. When writing your characters, do they have a physical limitation or a mental struggle that is so great that it affects their body and their movement?

Writing Rehearsal

- **What is your character's style? Choose a character from your work-in-progress and describe how they'd dress.**

- **What would they wear to impress someone on a date?**

- **What would they wear to a job interview?**

- **What would they choose as their favorite outfit?**

- **If they wore a concert t-shirt, which band would it be from?**

- **How does your character move? Do they have any unusual movements?**

Next, consider how your character speaks. The speed at which a character speaks can speak volumes. It could be slow because they are intoxicated or are composing a lie. It could be fast because they're nervous or come from a family where everyone always speaks at lightning speed. Depending on where the character was raised, they might have a dialect or use different phrases or terminology. Describing the pitch of their voice will help your readers create a more complete image of the character. Does the character have a speaking impediment? These are all characteristics of speech that a character might have. And there are endless more.

Another outer characteristic is physical ability. NFL MVP Patrick Mahomes can do things with a football that most people can't. He's trained and developed abilities that have taken him to the top of his field. This doesn't have to only pertain to sports. Perhaps the character is a very talented typist or piano player. Maybe they've won multiple awards for their knitting. There are endless physical abilities for characters. Find ones that your character has and *doesn't* have. If you are writing comedy, one of the best devices is putting a character in a situation where they don't have the skills or abilities to succeed. The famous character from the UK, Mr. Bean, always comes to mind here.

As an actor, I enjoy adding character ticks. These are unusual physical movements that make sense to that character. A person who's quit smoking might still frequently raise their hand to their mouth. An awkward teen at a new school might endlessly bite their cuticles. We all probably have seen someone tap their foot or flick a pen when they're bored or nervous. These are all ticks, and they can also lead your reader to know your characters more deeply.

Writing Rehearsal

Describe how your character speaks and moves.

- **Does your character have a dialect? If so, from what region?**

- **Does your character speak quickly or slowly?**

- **Are there times in your novel where the character's speech is affected by something like intoxication, a large wad of bubblegum, a gag, a forked tongue because they're a snake?**

- **What special movement skills does your character have or not have?**

- **Does your character have a tick? If so, what triggers it?**

Inner Elements

The outer elements of a character are what they see when they look in a mirror and what others notice about them when they're in the world. Their inner elements are the deeper, emotional aspects of the character. This area takes more work. You have to dig deeper. But by doing so, you'll create stronger character goals. These goals are what keep them going when they meet each of the crises you throw at them while writing their journey closer to the climax of your novel.

What is the one thing driving your character throughout your novel? If you don't know what they're trying to achieve, it's going to be difficult to write them through the challenges they're going to face. In Chapter 1, I mentioned that the overall conflict can be internal or external. Even if the conflict isn't solely internal, your characters are going to emotionally react to their challenges. And they're going to have thoughts and opinions on the outcomes they want in their story.

When creating the inner elements of a character, ask a lot of "why?" questions. Why questions open doors to the character's inner lives, so channel that three-year-old you know and start asking "why?" incessantly.

Also, center this around a big "what?" question. What does the character want above all else? Konstantin Stanislavsky is recognized as the singular person responsible for creating a realistic system for acting that is still being used today. He worked in Russia as a theatre director at the time of playwright Anton Chekhov. They often worked together in fact. What Stanislavsky did was create a method for developing a realistic style of acting. When he asked actors what their characters wanted above all else, he called that the superobjective. By defining your character's superobjective, you are giving them a driving force that will take them to the end of the book.

The superobjective is reflective of the inciting incident and the major dramatic question. Hamlet's superobjective is to avenge his father's death through the death of his uncle. It drives him to near insanity throughout the play. It affects every choice he makes and every response to a conflict that is thrown before him.

Just like with conflict, the superobjective is rooted in an inner or outer objective. It should be strong and specific. Weak superobjectives lead to weak conflict where readers stop reading and don't come back. Strong superobjectives lead to big conflict and readers turning pages for hours past their bedtimes.

Writing Rehearsal

- What is your main character or characters' superobjective? Be specific.

- Do you need to make the character's superobjective stronger? If so, how would you do this?

- What is it that drives them through the challenges in your novel?

We can thank Stanislavski for the frequent use of the word "specifics." He emphasized the importance of specifics heavily. For example, consider what a character is drinking. This can be their favorite drink, canned diet Coke, or a Starbucks drink with ten modifications. Specifics refer to all aspects of a character, including their goals.

Let's look at some examples. In a romance, the main character is looking for love. What kind of love? A love like her former fiance. Why isn't he around anymore? He was lost at sea from a crabbing boat in Alaska. How long ago did that happen? It's been five years.

See the specifics? She's not just looking for love, she's looking for a very specific kind of love.

In a thriller, there's always a bad guy, right? What makes him so bad? Maybe he's hunting down a police officer. Why a police officer? He blames this particular officer for destroying his life when the police officer impounded his car. Impounding a car isn't terrible right? What if due to not having a car, the bad guy lost his job, lost his wife, lost his kids, and lost his will to survive? Before he takes his own life, the bad guy wants to end the police officer's life.

This is much more specific than the bad guy just being a bad guy who makes bad choices.

Specifics are fantastic. They make your characters rich and layered with details that make them more realistic to your readers. Remember to be specific in describing both the inner and outer characteristics of your characters.

Writing Rehearsal

- List three specific descriptions of the outer elements of your character.

- List three specific descriptions of the inner elements of your character.

- Think about the superobjective you defined previously. Can you make your main character's superobjective more specific?

What? Why? How?

The last element of Stanislavsky's acting techniques I'd like to introduce you to is determining the what, why, and how of the character's actions. This gives your characters strong motivation and description of their actions and choices. For example, when I worked as a professional film and television extra in Los Angeles, I was a regular on CBS's *NCIS*. There I was an agent in the offices and often was given simple directions such as, "Walk around the outer area of the office in a clockwise direction." There was no purpose given to my movements, so I created those myself. I didn't have to, but as an actress, I chose to. It made it much more interesting for me as an actor, and hopefully for anyone who might have noticed me on the screen.

Stanislavsky said that actors should answer the questions about action on stage: What? Why? How?

When walking in circles around the office, I often imagined I'd lost my coffee somewhere. *What?* What was I doing? I was looking for my coffee with the last bit of caramel flavoring from the break room. *Why?* Why was I looking for my coffee? It'd been a late night where I'd stayed up too long chatting with a new guy I'd met on a dating app. *How?* How was I walking? I was walking briskly because I could not keep my eyes open standing up, so I was going to be in trouble when I had to sit down and listen to my supervisor drone on in our weekly meeting that starts in ten minutes.

What? Why? How? Answer these questions as you write scenes to describe the way your characters move through the story. Do you need to write a description of every movement the character makes? No. But if you are envisioning yourself as a character in a movie as you write, consider answering these questions. You might discover some delightful specifics that will add vivacity to your manuscript.

Let's take a deeper dive into character motivations by looking at how an actor justifies their character's actions on stage. Robert Cohen wrote an acting textbook where he coined the acronym GOTE. Goals. Obstacles. Tactics. Expectations.

When an actor defines these elements for their character, they do it in two manners. The first is to determine them for the overall play. The second is to determine them in each scene or possibly multiple times in the same scene as their character reacts to the world around them.

Goals

We've already talked about the superobjective. This is the overall goal that the character has throughout the entirety of the story. Yet, think about it within smaller scenes. For example, if a character we'll call Maxine has been kidnapped, she may have an ultimate goal of escape, but she might change her specific goals in reaction to the individual challenges she faces. In one scene, her goal might be to seduce her captor. In the next scene, her goal might be to incapacitate her captor.

Goals can, and do change from scene to scene, yet they should always support the superobjective.

Imagine a romance novel where the main character is named Sophie. Her goal is to marry before she turns thirty. Every scene might have a new goal that ultimately leads to her either succeeding or not. But if there is a random scene thrown in about her auditioning for a reality TV singing competition but it has nothing to do with her superobjective (marriage before thirty), then that's a scene to cut.

Obstacles

With every goal must come an obstacle, something preventing the character from reaching their goal. What stands in the character's way preventing them from succeeding? This could be a physical (outer) obstacle or an emotional (inner) obstacle. Using the example above, Maxine might have the goal of seducing her captor. A physical obstacle could be that she's tied to a chair. Can she still seduce her captor? Absolutely! But it's much more challenging, and therefore interesting to your readers to see this obstacle. For an inner obstacle, Maxine might struggle with confidence and doesn't believe that she can seduce anyone, let alone the person who's kidnapped her.

Obstacles build the intensity of the conflict. And the more conflict, the more interesting the story will be to your readers. The obstacles should intensify as the conflict grows. Remember that you are starting at the bottom of the hill with Freytag's Pyramid.

As the character fights to go up that hill they will encounter new and bigger challenges that push them to their limit.

In comedy, this can lead to a level of what I call comic ridiculousness. Comedies generally start within an element of reality. The reader should be able to connect to the characters by believing the situation they're in. But as the conflict grows, so can the ridiculousness. If you've captured your reader with the character and the character's journey, they'll overlook more and more ridiculousness and buy into the story. This is why some of the funniest books end with some of the craziest endings.

Tactics

If you are walking across the street to buy a cup of coffee at the local coffee store, the coffee you absolutely need to make it through the morning, but a dog jumps into your path, what do you do? Goal: coffee. Obstacle: dog. What you do is the tactic, the action that you take to overcome the obstacle. Your characters will need tactics to reach their goals in the face of obstacles too.

One character might be a dog lover who befriends the dog, giving it copious belly rubs, and bringing it home. Another character might be afraid of dogs and walk all the way down the block to cross the street and double back to get their coffee. An evil character or villain will just pepper spray the dog and whistle as they strut to the coffee shop.

Who the character is as a person (or other being) will determine their tactics. With each obstacle, the character will change their tactics. Maybe the obstacle is a dog. Maybe a car racing from the police. Maybe a pushy salesperson. Maybe a wizard with the power to end the world. With each different obstacle, your characters must choose how they face it. Will they overcome with a battle of wits or brute power? Will they avoid it or run away? Will they wilt under the pressure or rise to face it? These are all questions to contemplate with each challenge you throw at your characters.

When actors determine their tactics, they often apply an action verb to their choice. There are long lists of acting verbs that can be found online. Here is a short list: lure, seduce, overpower, entertain, convince, destroy, badger, heal, inspire, warn, shun, alert, and many, many more. When using these verbs consider if the character is trying to pull someone in or push them away. That's a quick place to start, then specify, specify, specify until you find the right tactic acting verb for that scene.

Remember: Tactics do not stay the same throughout the character's journey. They change with each new scene or obstacle.

Expectations

This element is the icing on the cake. You've determined the obstacle, the goal, and the tactic. But what does your character expect will happen when they deploy their tactic? When I was in high school, I volunteered at a blood drive held at our school. One of the nurses told me to look out for the football players. They always give blood then hop up really quickly, take two steps, and faint. While this was humorous to my awkward teen girl self, it's a wonderful example of character expectations. The football players expected that they would give blood and be totally fine. What was humorous was that their expectations were totally wrong.

No one faces an obstacle without creating a story in their mind of how they expect it to end. Some of the greatest books, films, and plays based on real people and events star characters who faced insurmountable obstacles they didn't expect to overcome. But the fact that they did overcome them is what makes the stories fascinating. Audiences love underdogs and overcomers.

How does this apply to a thriller? Remember Maxine, the character who was kidnapped and tied to a chair? Her goal is to escape. Her obstacle is that her hands are tied behind her. Her tactic might be to seduce her captor. Her expectation might be that she will lure him close enough to head butt him, knock him unconscious, and find a way to grab the knife strapped to his belt.

How does this apply to a romance? Violet is at the hospital where she works as a nurse. Her shift is over and her parents are expecting her at their 40th anniversary dinner. Her goal is to leave the hospital. But in rushes Elijah, one of the paramedics. He's out of uniform and carrying a young girl with a crudely bandaged arm. Her obstacle appears when she locks eyes with Elijah. Her heart flutters as her brain reminds her that her parents never permit tardiness and they've been planning this party for over a year. What does she do? Her tactic is to help Elijah, telling herself she's doing it for the girl crying in his arms. Her expectation is that she can get Elijah to notice her if she helps him and the girl and if she does it fast enough, she'll only be two minutes late to her parent's party.

What happens next is the rest of the story. Does the character succeed? This is what readers want to know. It's what keeps them turning the pages. Remember from Chapter 1 that your characters should fluctuate between winning and losing. This both builds tension and gives your reader moments to cheer on the characters.

Writing Rehearsal

Pick one scene from your WIP and answer the following questions with specific answers.

- What is the character's goal?

- What is the character's obstacle?

- What is the character's tactic to overcome the obstacle?

- What is the character's expectation?

Character Secret

Who doesn't love a good secret? Readers certainly do. And so do actors. A trick actors use to bring an extra level of realism to their characters is to create a secret. This is not something given to them directly from the text, but something they (as artists) create based on the script.

Here's an example of a character secret I used when I was in graduate school. In an acting class, I was in a group with friends to rehearse and perform a scene from Anton Chekhov's The Three Sisters. In it, I played Olga, the oldest sister who was unmarried. Maria was the middle sister who was married but didn't really care for her husband. And Irina, the youngest, was looking for her true love. It's a wonderful play with rich characters. But I wanted to add another layer to my character as Olga.

Konstantin Stanislavsky worked with Chekhov frequently, so I applied one of Stanislavsky's acting tricks. Ask yourself, "What if... ?" For this scene, I asked myself, "What if Olga was secretly in love with Maria's husband?" As soon as I did this, I had a whole new world for my character. When Maria would complain about her husband, I (as Olga) would become annoyed. When Maria's husband came into the room, I would sneak glances at him. Every choice I made was different now that I imagined that Olga was in love with her sister's husband.

When writing your characters, think about a secret they might carry. What's fun with character secrets is that you don't have to tell anyone your secret. I didn't until after our final performance. The secret your character(s) carry should be based on their past experiences affecting how they interact with the world of your manuscript. You might consider revealing your character's secret to your readers.

This is where I step out of my acting box and into my author box. Revelations are different in a literary world where the reader is given access to character's inner thoughts. These secrets can be revealed at opportune moments such as when an emotional connection is made between two characters or as a way to build empathy for a villain. The big, juicy secrets might be revealed at the climax of your story too. Who can forget Darth Vader's world-altering words as a one-handed Luke Skywalker clung on for life? You know those words. Big secret. Big reveal. Big moment for the audience to gasp in surprise.

Writing Rehearsal

- Think about possible secrets for your main character and supporting characters.

- Brainstorm ideas for how these secrets the characters carry affect their interaction in the world.

- Decide if, how, and when these secrets will be revealed in your manuscript.

Chapter 3
THEME

BECAUSE ARISTOTLE DIDN'T WRITE in English, his work has been translated. For this element, it has been translated as "theme" or "thought." Essentially, it's the overall message or thought you want to leave with your readers. Recently, I read *The Measure* by Nikki Erlick. The premise of this book (knowing the length of your life) led to so many themes. They each made me think deeply and consider my own worldview. In the end, I was greatly moved by this novel. Themes can do that for your readers.

Many themes are found in literature, the theatre, film, and anywhere stories are told. A theme helps you focus your story on a grander idea. Your story isn't simply boy meets girl. With a theme it becomes boy meets girl as they overcome big business trying to invade small towns and destroy local economy. When a murderer is on the loose and a young detective is on the hunt, add a theme and the young detective is overcoming the trauma of being a neglected child as they understand the killer in a way no one else can.

There are some common themes used by writers, themes in their basest forms: mankind vs. mankind, mankind vs. nature, and mankind vs. themself. These are the most simple forms of themes. When evaluating the theme, consider what the main character is fighting for and what is keeping them from their goal. If you are unsure of the theme in your book, this will help you define it.

There are many more themes that are found in literature, themes revolving around love, war, justice, family, the meaning of life, and good vs. evil. Themes add a message to your story, something for your readers to learn or a place to discover. Choose a theme for your book that readers will connect with. In my debut novel, an overarching theme was two characters with new disabilities learning how to live in new ways and showing their community they still had value. It was a rustic community that wanted to banish them both simply because of their disabilities.

When exploring themes consider internal and external themes. External themes can resonate in the world surrounding the character. In my novel, there are vicious beasts roaming the forest that hunt on the villagers. It's a theme of survival for both humans and beasts. Other external themes might include nature, the broken world, man vs. man, and many more.

Internal themes come from inside the character, based on a struggle from within. In my novel, the internal theme was the characters learning to live with their disabilities as they learned about the true meaning of love. They couldn't interact with the world as before and were both overcoming broken dreams for a future they could no longer reach. Other internal themes might include generational curses, overcoming addiction, self-esteem, familial expectations, and many more.

Some authors will start a novel with a theme in mind. Other authors might discover the theme popping up more and more the deeper they dive into the script. Both of these experiences are valid. I'd compare this to Stephen King's comparison of authors who prefer to plan all elements of their novels with those who sit down and write by the seat of their pants. What's important is that, as an author, you decide if you want a specific theme or what themes develop during your writing process.

Another way you could look at theme, is to compare your book to a birthday party. Is the birthday party like the one my daughter requested for her 13th birthday party? If so, it's Taylor Swift themed, celebrated at a local cat cafe, and has an after-party with a shopping spree at the mall. The theme of this party is centered around everything a 13-year-old loves. Other birthday parties might be like the dour office party with the saddest rendition of the happy birthday song found in the film *Office Space*.

Just like birthday parties have themes so do books. Maybe a birthday party theme is more noticeable than a book's theme, but it's still there. Find it. Define it. Share it with your readers.

Writing Rehearsal

- What themes are found in your WIP?

- Are these themes internal or external? How so?

- If your book had a birthday party, what kind of theme would it be?

I'd like to shift gears here and discuss genre, which is lightly connected to theme. Theme is the overarching message, but genre is the method in which the message is conveyed. For example, the theme is the destination for a road trip but the genre is the mode of transportation that gets someone to the destination.

A common symbol of the theatre is the two drama masks indicating comedy and tragedy. These are the most basic genres. Even Shakespeare's plays are separated into these categories along with the histories that tell the stories of leaders in the monarchy. The theme of your novel will help guide it toward its genre. Is it a comedy or a tragedy? A professor once told me that you know the difference in Shakespeare's plays because in comedies everyone gets married at the end and in tragedies everyone dies in the end.

The best way to determine the genre of your manuscript is to ask yourself where it would sit on a bookshelf at the bookstore. Romance? Thriller? Young Adult? Non-Fiction? Horror? Fantasy? Science Fiction? Historical Fiction?

Once you determine the genre, you can consider the sub-genres. Those are endless. But they are great for helping your readers get a clearer understanding of your novel. I've seen fantasy books that are romantic fantasy, horror fantasy, or contemporary fantasy. Subgenres are great for clarifying the theme of your manuscript.

Some authors have asked about blending genres. While this is exciting for artists, it may be difficult for marketing. If you have an established base of readers, you can do almost anything you want. Look at writing giants like James Patterson, Colleen Hoover, or Stephen King. Their readers are so dedicated they'll read anything in any genre that these authors write. If you are just getting started on your writing journey, you might consider sticking to a clear genre until you can build the audience you want. But at the end of the day, blaze your own trail whether that's following other's experiences or off-roading on your own wild adventure.

A writer friend and I had a long discussion once because she wasn't sure exactly what genre her manuscript fell into, romance or women's fiction. She primarily wrote suspense but had greatly enjoyed writing a lighter-hearted manuscript she was pitching as a rom-com. Determining the exact genre of your manuscript based on industry standards can be a challenge. The best advice I was given was to read many books in the genre I write. By going to the bookstore or library and reading books from the industry-assigned genres, you'll notice themes and trends that you can compare to your manuscript.

Connecting with groups of writers in your genre can be very useful. I've found that often other writers have wonderful ideas and at times very direct, useful criticism. The best writing group will encourage you and push you to be your best. Find a local group or one online. Also, find fellow writers in your genre on social media. Yes, social media is huge and overwhelming at times. But, I've discovered a lot of encouragement and celebration in online author groups. And there's a lot of shared information that I've found extremely useful.

Writing Rehearsal

- Where would your book be found on a shelf in a bookstore?

- What subgenres are found in your novel?

- What books have you read or want to read in your genre?

- Find a writing group in your area or online that you could visit.

Chapter 4
LANGUAGE

THIS SECTION THAT ARISTOTLE identified is often called "language" or "diction." It's how the character communicates. Not just the methodology but also the words the character uses. As an actor, when I've analyzed a script and built a character I've put a lot of thought and work into determining the language of the character. Of course, in a play, the character's lines are given to the actor by the playwright. As an author, you get to consider the words the character uses when they speak and how they say them. When determining the language of your characters, I encourage you to consider location, education, personality, and the situation.

Location

Where a person grows up influences their language. Just ask people from other parts of the country if they say "soda" or "pop" when talking about carbonated beverages. Then enjoy a chuckle when someone tells you they call everything "Coke." This is a silly example, but a good one about regional words. Where the character is from will affect the words they use to describe things. When researching, consider finding ways to discover these regionalisms. With access to so many videos online, it should be easy to find people from specific areas speaking in their native manner.

Also, consider the dialect. Recently, I was listening to an audio-book where a character was from Vermont, but the narrator used a Southern accent. I was immediately confused. His language didn't match how his character had been described. It pulled me out of the story because I was trying to figure out if I'd heard something wrong or if it was just a poor acting choice.

In the United States, there are multiple dialects, just as in other countries. As an actor, I studied these American and foreign dialects and became a dialect coach. The beautiful thing about dialects is that they can quickly inform the audience or reader of that character's roots. Dialects can be difficult to write, so do so with care. One of the reasons Margaret Mitchell's *Gone with the Wind* was a sensation was that she wrote the character's dialogue with their dialect. It brought new life and vivacity to the book. Readers could see the words and hear how they sounded from the page.

Consider if a character races into a room holding a large, flopping fish. You'll know what part of the country they're in based what they say, "Dude, this fish is like, so crazy huuuge!" Or "Ah, jeez, this fella's a whopper, don't ya know?" Word choices and dialect can instantly draw your readers into the world you are creating.

Education

The level of education a person has completed often affects their vocabulary. It's not always true, but generally, a person who is well-read and educated will have a more wide and diverse vocabulary. This is important to remember when writing characters that are children. When children use words uncommon for children, it can become humorous. When my daughter was four years old her favorite word was "treacherous." We laugh about it as a family. She was my firstborn, and I didn't know that children her age didn't use such big words. But she did. Having a large vocabulary was and continues to be part of her character. This is influenced by her access to books and likely because both her parents have post-graduate degrees. We love all the words and have never held back from using big words in front of our kids.

When writing a character, if they speak in a way that is not reflective of their education level it will come off as awe-inspiring or humorous. When considering education, keep in mind that this means more than the level of grades or degrees completed. A person might not graduate high school but be an avid reader who reads all kinds of books. This character would also have a higher vocabulary because they have educated themselves.

Also, consider other kinds of education that affect vocabulary. Every job has its own vocabulary. Whether it's a nurse or a librarian or an electrician, they will use terms that aren't common to others. And consider other kinds of education like street smarts. This is another area that has its own unique vocabulary that helps your reader know your characters more deeply.

Personality

When building characters, it's good practice to observe people. I've pulled many little details from observations that I've added to my writing. Why? Because people are fascinating and you always find something new.

How people express themselves is unique in every way. As authors, we have the privilege of creating characters that are equally unique. A character's personality determines what words they'll use in conversation. If they are formal and dressed to kill every day they'll likely speak more formally. If they're a teenager wearing torn jeans and a baggy t-shirt they might speak in monosyllabic grunts. Personality can also affect their speaking speed and rhythms. There will be more on this in Chapter 5: Music.

Variations are also useful when determining a character's language. Think about the major and secondary characters in your manuscript. Do they all speak the same? If they're all from the same area, they might have a similar dialect, but how do education and personality create differences across the characters? Finding variations of language in characters is like having a visually pleasing painting. If everyone acts and talks the same, it's like painting in only one color. When variations are added, you can use all the colors of the rainbow.

Another part of a person's personality is the challenges they face and overcome daily. For example, does your character have a speech impediment? Having a stutter or a lisp is a rich characteristic. But use this only when necessary. In the past, giving a character a speech impediment was done almost solely for comedy, making implications that the character was ignorant. This assumption was wrong. And I'm glad that writers are veering away from such hurtful associations. A lot of this is due to people speaking out.

National Youth Poet Laureate Amanda Gorman speaks openly about her struggle with stuttering. When writing her poetry, she admits to choosing words that were easier for her to say to avoid public embarrassment. So, if you add a speech impediment to your character, that can be okay. Just be sure that it's an honest representation and, if used for comedy, the speech impediment isn't the only humorous element of the character.

Situation

There are theories I've read about how people wear masks. If they are at work, they wear their work mask. At home, their home mask. This will affect a character's speech too. I don't know about you, but I have a "phone voice." After working in office jobs and as a receptionist, I developed my happy, perky, "so glad you called" voice. I used this voice when I spoke with kind people and when I spoke with angry, entitled people who called my office. I'll admit here that I also have a high-pitched, happy voice I use when I talk to my cats. They couldn't care less, but in my mind, that voice helps me show my true adoration for my cats. Now, when they puke on the carpet, I use a very different voice. Yuck.

Situations can change how we speak as humans. These could be simple situations such as changing the masks we wear but can vary when something new is thrust upon us. This can be as simple as a character stumbling over their words when they meet the most beautiful person in the world. Or it can be as complicated as a character struggling to recall exactly the passcode for the nuclear launch as the barrel of a gun presses into their temple.

Another situation to consider is inebriation. If a character is drunk, high, or has an illness or injury that affects their ability to form words, this is a situation that will change the words they use and how they speak them. It also gives characters a freer tongue to say things they might not normally say out loud. Sure, Aunt Gladys looks ridiculous in her tight, bright, flower print dress at Grandpa Joe's funeral. But only someone inebriated, or who wants to be in the casket for the next funeral, would dare say anything to her about it.

Writing Rehearsal

Think about a character that you've created or plan to create and answer the following questions. This can be repeated for the major and secondary characters.

- Where was the character raised? Where do they live now?

- What level of education does the character have? How does this influence their language?

- What about the character's personality affects their language?

- Is there any situation in your WIP where the character would be inebriated?

Chapter 5
MUSIC

DURING THE GREEK ERA of theatre, Aristotle recognized the importance of music. The performers included a chorus that sang sections of the play. Their function was to provide expository information and inform the audience of plot changes between act and scene breaks. It wasn't quite like a modern musical but closer to that than a standard play. Because music was used by the chorus to inform the audience, Aristotle included it in his six elements of the drama.

When considering the function of music in literature as it was used by the Greeks, we can look at the presentation of expository information. Outside of basic plot construction, this is commonly seen when a sequel is written and the author has to inform new readers what's happening in the story in case they didn't read the previous book or books. Beyond expository information, music in literature can be described best as pacing and rhythm.

Pacing

Pacing in books can be overlooked. When writing, we authors should force ourselves to look at how we construct sentences, paragraphs, and chapters. Picture book writers have some of the biggest challenges when constructing these. They must make every word, every punctuation count because they have such a small word count to work with.

When writing for younger readers, it's common to use simpler language and shorter, less complex sentences. When writing for teen and adult audiences, writers don't have to write in this manner. There is more freedom to vary the way a story is constructed. The age and reading ability of the targeted readers should be considered when setting the pace. In general, the younger a reader, the shorter their attention span, thus the shorter the sentences, paragraphs, chapters, etc.

Literary fiction has its own world of beauty in sentence construction. Words are chosen carefully, sentences are built like they were designed by an architect. This flow of words pulls the reader into the world of the story. Writers of fantasy also create worlds carefully when creating names of characters and beings that are unfamiliar to readers.

Writers of all genres should also focus on how they construct a scene. I've read books I loved but the chapters were so long it was difficult to complete. I would try to get to a good stopping point but give up. I'm just one reader, but when writing, consider the shortened attention span of many readers today. You have to hook them and keep them on the line. By structuring your story with varied lengths of sentences, paragraphs, and chapters, you can keep them turning pages and not putting your book aside to collect dust.

A rule I follow when considering pace in my writing is: The faster a character's heart beats, the quicker the pace should be. Our hearts race when we're nervous, excited, terrified, or sexually stimulated. In scenes where the character's heartbeat is quick, write with shorter sentences and paragraphs. If the character's heart rate is slow in the scene, the pacing can be slower too. This means longer, more descriptive sentences that paint a lush world for the reader.

Outside of the structure of the sentences, paragraphs, and chapters, there should be variety in the amount of dialogue and narration. Dialogue, when the characters are speaking, can be engaging but readers lose interest if there isn't narration to color the world of the book and share the character's inner thoughts.

As an actor who has worked often with play scripts, I am guilty of writing lengthy dialogue scenes. I'm talking about pages and pages of dialogue and very little narration. And it's terrible. Even editing it I get lost in the forest of quotation marks. At moments like this, I'm grateful for editing.

Narration in your writing doesn't have to be complex. Dropping in a dialogue tag with a description of a character's movement can add insight into their inner life.

For example: *"I've never seen you in the library before."* This sentence alone gives a location and the impression that the character speaking is surprised. Let's add some narration.

"I've never seen you in the library before," Chloe tucked a loose tendril of hair behind her ear, her teeth nibbling on her lower lip.

By adding the narration, we know the character's name, her physical ticks, and have an impression of her emotional state. The narration fills out the world of the manuscript and gives insight into the inner thoughts of the characters. Find the rhythm in your manuscript by balancing dialogue and narration.

Warning: When adding dialog tags, be sure to show not tell. This is a common term in acting that I've also seen over and over again in writing lessons. In the example above, the author doesn't tell the audience that Chloe is nervous. The reader knows that Chloe is nervous by her actions, nibbling on her lower lip. When editing, look for moments where you might fall into telling your reader something and see if you can show them instead.

Writing Rehearsal

Pull a page or two from your WIP and highlight the narration in one color and the dialogue in another. (I would count inner dialogue and thoughts as dialogue too.) Do this on paper or digitally. It can give you a quick visual representation of the rhythm of your scene.

- What do you see?

- Is the pace where you want it to be?

- If not, what can you change to improve the pacing of this scene?

I'd be a terrible theatre teacher if I didn't take a moment to discuss playwright David Mamet and his use of rhythm. When I was a grad student in the early 2000s, Mamet was all the rage, and rightly so. He writes plays using beats written specifically into the playscript that affect the rhythm of the performances on stage. What is a "beat?" Similar to a beat in music, it's a rest. In theatre, it's a moment to take a breath. Or a longer beat is a moment for the character to think or choose their words.

How can a beat work in literature? Commonly, authors write an ellipsis or a dash to show a break or change in a character's dialogue. A dash shows a quick stop while an ellipsis shows a longer break. Also, don't forget those commas. They are little beats in dialogue and even in narration.

As an acting teacher, I taught my students how to perform a "cold read" audition. This is when the actor is thrust in front of the director, often with a partner, and given a script to read on the spot. They're supposed to perform the scene sight unseen using emotion and interpretation of the script. Sound like a daunting task? It is! But there are some tricks to developing cold reading skills. The most important one is to use the punctuation given by the playwright. A period is a hard stop. A comma is a brief, quick pause. Exclamation marks and question marks inform the actor of the meaning or intensity of the lines.

A fun practice to test your pacing is to try a cold read of your manuscript. As you workshop scenes and even present them to critique partners, try reading them out loud. For some writers, reading their work out loud is as emotionally painful as a root canal is physically painful. Try it anyway. But if this is anxiety-inducing, find a safe space for this activity. Find the people who will build you up and encourage you. And if even that feels impossible, try reading to a pet or a stuffed animal. This might sound silly, but I have often rehearsed lines working on my memorization speaking to my cat. And the best thing is that my cat wasn't any more judgmental about my writing than they were about anything else.

By reading your manuscript out loud, you will find where little parts don't work and places where the flow is interrupted. And the best part is that you'll find places where it does work! You'll find those places where you have to stop and tell yourself that what you just read was beautiful, a work of art. And you wrote that!

Lastly, have fun writing the pacing like this. In my YA novel *Junior Year Bites*, I had the best time writing a comic character that everyone loves to hate. At one point another character asks him to count to ten. He responds with heavy snark spouting, "Onetwothreefourfivesixseveneightnineten!" I put a quick bit of narration in there too to describe how the words rolled off his tongue. See how the words are smashed together possibly confusing the reader. Yes, I allowed my readers to scratch their heads briefly in confusion for a moment. As an artist, I felt it was worth it because comedy is quick, and having the character speak this way tells the reader more about the character than I can in narration.

Writing Rehearsal

Try reading a few pages of your manuscript out loud. Do it in a safe space. Don't try to use AI or have Word read it to you because these programs won't capture the nuances and emotion of your writing. Read it yourself. And if you want to take it to a new level, record yourself (audio or video) and enjoy reviewing the playback.

 For authors, there are more lessons to be learned from the Greek choruses of Aristotle's day. The chorus, similar to a chorus today, was a group of people performing together in unison. In Aristotle's day, the chorus would have included approximately fifteen to fifty people. The purpose of the Greek chorus was to provide information to the audience.

Imagine a Greek theatre for a moment. They were outdoors with shows performed only during the daylight. If the scene in the play took place at night, the chorus would describe the "night" as they set the beginning of a scene. The chorus also provides other necessary expository information such as a change in time or location.

One unique characteristic of Greek theatre was that they did not show violence on stage. (Later with the Romans all kinds of violence was shown!) For example, in the play *Oedipus Rex*, the title character is so distraught to learn how a choice made earlier in his life has affected his current situation that he gouges out his own eyes. Yep, it's gross. If you don't know the play, you can look up the plot and see what happens. Here's a hint: It's from this play that psychologists coined the term "oedipal complex."

How was this handled on a Greek stage? The chorus tells the audience what Oedipus has done. fter their descriptions and setting the scene, Oedipus was led onstage wearing his character mask, but this one would show blood dripping down his cheeks.

When writing, especially when you start a new chapter or scene where the location, time, or situation has changed, think about the Greek chorus. Have you shared this information with your audience? I know that when I write, I'm guilty of creating the world so strongly in my mind that I forget to write into my WIP these kinds of details. It's left some of my beta readers asking me how my characters got from one point to another. When working with beta readers, it's great to ask them if they notice things like this.

In theatre, the actors perform the words from their scripts for the audience to hear. These words can set the scene in various ways. Even in Shakespeare's day, plays were performed in the daylight. Shakespeare wrote into his plays what I call verbal scenery. The audience knows it's nighttime in *Romeo and Juliet* because Romeo speaks of the beauty of the moon and compares it to Juliet.

I point this out because authors have it a little easier. We can write into the narration the beauty of the moon. But our characters can talk about it too. The two important takeaways from this section are: (1) Whatever the scene, if there's been a change be sure that you inform your audience of that, and (2) Use your artistic ability to paint your scenes using a mixture of dialogue and narration. Maybe you write in the narration that it's night, but a character comments on being cold. That gives you the time of day and the weather.

Writing Rehearsal

Study how you've written expository information. Look at a scene or chapter in your WIP.

- Read the first page or two and see if you've conveyed to your audience the time, location, weather, change in location, etc.

- Or ask a critique partner or beta reader to read it for you and underline any mention of expository information.

- Or do both!

For further study and exploration, look at how other writers have set their scenes. At a library or a bookstore, flip through the first pages of a book and see what information you can garner in the first page or two. Don't be afraid to look at classics from theatre such as Shakespeare and the playwrights from the Greek and Roman eras.

Chapter 6
SPECTACLE

THE FINAL ELEMENT OF the drama, and the least important according to Aristotle, is spectacle. This refers to the visual and technical elements of the play. In Aristotle's day, this meant primarily the costumes, masks, and varied sets or special effects. In Greek theatre, costumes were simple. Masks were worn by the performers. They designated their roles in the play and could be changed for different scenes to show varied emotions or other characteristics.

When it came to the sets, they weren't much compared to today's Western theatre. The theatres were built with permanent stage settings that could indicate common locations such as a palace or a city square. A common special effect was the deus ex machina. Translated to English, it means "god from a machine." What might happen in a play would be that the playwright would write themselves into a corner and need an easy way out. Enter the Greek gods. At these points, a machine system with an arm would bring an actor playing one of the gods onstage. It lifted them up and over the back wall (or skene) of the stage. The god then used their supernatural powers to solve the problem of the play.

In writing, the term deus ex machina is also used. Writers (including myself) have written themselves into a corner where they can't find a way out for their characters. In fantasy, this can be solved with some kind of magic or a fantastical animal's arrival. They show up and, like the Greek god, solve the problems. In a thriller, an example would be the police officer randomly discovering the final piece of evidence in a manner that feels a little too easy.

In writing, some authors call a deus ex machina a cheap trick. It is an easy way out, and if you're on deadline, it's a quicker choice than going back and changing multiple points in your novel. Whether a deus ex machina in literature is a good choice or not is debatable. If you'd like to read more about other's thoughts on this subject, a simple online search of "deus ex machina in writing" will provide you with many sources because this device is used in all areas of writing including novels, plays, television, and film.

Because there wasn't a strong focus on the spectacle elements of Greek plays, Aristotle put it at the bottom of his list. If he were alive today, I believe he would put spectacle much higher. From Broadway to local community theatres, much effort is put into designing and building the set, designing and building the costumes, designing the lights, and coordinating all the sound elements.

When writing, we need to envision the world of our characters. This includes the setting, the clothing, the effects of the environment, and lighting.

The Setting

The setting of a novel is important. It can be simply broken down by asking questions much like a scene designer will ask questions of a script before starting their design. The first questions are those answered by the exposition. The visual world will vary depending on the location, time, economic status of the characters, etc.

Beyond the exposition questions, a simple first question is: interior or exterior? Does the action take place indoors or outdoors? While many people already have answers to these simple questions when writing, it's a good place to start for those who don't have a good feel for the scene yet. When you start with broad questions, you can keep specifying until you have a clear scene created in your mind.

The more specific you are, the easier it will be to write. For example, let's say you're writing a scene that takes place in a cabin at a sleepaway camp in rural Iowa. It's a church camp that the main character has visited each summer for the past six years, but now they're in college and working as a camp counselor.

What does the cabin look like? Is it made of cinder blocks or wood? Does it have air conditioning or a ceiling fan? What are the windows like? Are they open-air with screens? How many people share the room with the main character? How many beds are there? Are they bunk beds? Do the beds have squeaky springs?

Answering questions like this can help you color the scene in your mind before your characters interact with it. Also, the genre of your manuscript will determine more specific elements of your scene. If the example above is in a horror novel, there might be strips of fly paper hanging throughout the room clustered with dead flies and strange stains streak the hard-wood floors. That's not a very welcoming environment. If the cabin is in a fantasy novel, there might be an open window for the servant fairies to fly through and the sound of zipsling bugs chirping in the sunlight outside. Same cabin, different details. Specifics matter.

What do you do when you can't picture the scene? Being a visual learner, I often either base a scene on a real place or find one online. For one book I wrote, I based the main character's house on a lovely butter-yellow house a few blocks from my daughter's elementary school. Every time I drive be it now, I smile and think of my characters. For a current WIP, one location is in Baton Rouge, Louisiana. I've only been to Baton Rouge once and that was just driving through. I went online and found maps, pictures, and real estate listings. Again, I based the location of a few scenes on real places. The house where some of the characters live is based on a house I found listed for sale. I was able to look at the size of the house and pictures of all the rooms in the listing. Later, when I wrote a scene where a main character enters the kitchen, I could easily describe the setting. I've had other writer friends who've used popular map sites with street views to virtually walk down a street an ocean away and write that into their manuscripts.

Writing Rehearsal

- Determine the specific setting of a scene in your WIP.

- Is it based on a real location? If yes, describe it or obtain pictures of the location.

- Is it something you've created? If yes, find photos or on-line resources to make that scene realistic with details.

Lighting

A scene's setting matters very much. As authors, it's our job to create that scene in our minds thoroughly so we can communicate that rich environment to our readers. One element that can significantly affect the scene is the lighting. When I was an undergrad, my lighting design teacher's name was Jerry. He was strict but loving and pushed us to do our best. When designing a show, the changes in lights are called cue changes. For the final project in Jerry's class, we each had to design the lights for one-act plays directed by students in the directing class. I spent many late nights in the theatre hanging, focusing, and programming lights, but in the end, I had my 32 light cues programmed into the lighting board and incorporated the use of a scrim (a gauze-like fabric used for lighting effects). The lighting looks I created had to evoke various emotions from the audience from joy to horror. Lighting can do that in books too.

In theatre, the lighting can be manipulated in many ways such as intensity, direction, color, and with some lights the shape or pattern. A scene with lower intensity and blue lights will create the feeling of being outside at night or underwater. A scene with brighter lights and warm colors will create the feeling of being in the sunshine. Designers change the lights to affect the mood of the play. They manipulate the scene just as an author can. Many intimate scenes in novels take place in settings where the space is small and the lighting is darker. Authors might not be thinking specifically about how lighting affects their scenes, but in our souls, we can feel the emotions created in those scenes. And we can help bring our readers deeper into the the world of the novel by adding even a small descriptor of the lighting.

When describing the scene and the lighting, keep in mind how the weather affects the scene. How many romance movies involve the love interests kissing in the rain? Or in a dimly lit location? Or stuck alone in a tiny room? In my opinion, these settings create an intimate space because they make the world feel smaller to the characters. There is nothing in the world but the person in front of them. The rain keeps them from leaving and the sound of it hitting the roof muffles any other sounds. In dimmer or dark light, people might feel more willing to share parts of themselves they wouldn't in the light.

Consider how weather can affect the lighting and mood of your scene. When a little girl starts at a new school with an evil head-mistress, the skies are cloudy as she walks through the gate for the first time. Or when a young man survives a night of deadly tornados that destroy his home, he might stop for a moment to soak in the morning sun shining on his face as he emerges from the rubble.

The weather might set the scene or work in opposition to it. A wonderful example of working in opposition is the famous dance scene from the film *Singin' in the Rain*. Gene Kelley's character is so happy that the rain can't keep him down.

Writing Rehearsal

Pick a scene in your WIP.

- Describe how lighting could play a role in the scene.

- How does lighting reflect the emotion you are capturing in the scene?

- Does the weather affect the scene?

- If you are not reaching your desired emotional level in the scene, is there something you can add about the lighting to capture it?

Costumes

Our final visual element of spectacle is costumes. The clothes people wear send a message. That message could be something as simple as the person's occupation. When going to work, a construction worker dresses differently than a doctor or a teacher. If you're writing a scene about a doctor who is fidgety, you might include them flicking the stethoscope hanging around their neck. A construction worker might laugh when they drop a hammer on their toes. It doesn't hurt so bad when you wear steel-toed boots. A fun way to add personal expression to a character is to have them in a traditional work uniform and add flair. A doctor wearing a clown nose is likely a pediatrician. A teacher wearing a nice black shirt with black pants that have streaks of various paint colors might be a high school drama teacher coming in from painting a set. The doctor and the teacher wear clothes appropriate to their occupation but with a twist reflecting their personality.

People also choose their clothing based on the occasion. A middle-aged woman will choose different clothes for her son's soccer game vs. her co-worker's wedding. A guy in college will choose different clothes for an 8:00 a.m. class versus a date with the hottest girl on campus. The reason a character gets dressed also affects their choices.

Outside of uniforms or strictly regimented clothing such as in the military, humans many, many clothing choices. Consider the practical elements in choosing clothes such as the weather and our exposure to it. On a hot summer day, people wear less clothes than on a cold winter day.

Think about how your characters would dress. Do they follow the norms and expectations, or not? When I lived overseas in Asia we worked with a group of guys from Minnesota. Culturally in our city, it was expected that everyone wear many layers in cold weather. This is why the grannies at the vegetable stand squawked and chastised the guys from Minnesota for wearing shorts in 40-degree weather. To that group of guys, it was a normal choice. The cold didn't bother them. But to those grannies, it was unthinkable because those boys would surely become ill from the cold.

Weather affects clothing choice, as does culture. In strictly religious cultures, much exposure of skin is forbidden while in some places in Europe, it's the opposite perspective. The culture and its values determine the clothing characters wear. In the United States, we have a blend of many cultures. Sometimes they clash, sometimes they learn to accept each other. So if you're looking to create conflict, this could be an easy way to do it. Imagine the conflict between parents and teens when picking "appropriate" clothes for the new school year.

Within cultures, there are also styles of clothing. Some of these are practical, related to the weather and protecting oneself from it. Others are influenced by the history and revival of certain styles. More yet reflect subgroups in a culture that bubble to the top. Glam rock of the 1970s and 1980s influenced styles across Europe and the United States. From Japan arose the Harajuku style from the Harajuku district of Tokyo, a center for fashion. Its root influence is from Japanese school uniforms.

Functionality and comfort should also be considered for a character's clothing. Anyone who's experienced plantar fasciitis like myself will avoid wearing high heels or dress shoes at all costs. I live in running shoes. My nephew is a long-distance runner on scholarship at a university. He practically lives in running shoes too, just for different reasons. We don't choose running shoes for style, it's for comfort and functionality. In Jojo Moyes' *Someone Else's Shoes,* the plot is centered around a pair of high-heeled shoes and what they mean to two different women.

Many comic scenes have been written where a character has to wear clothing that is too small or too large. Any person who's worn a tight skirt and tried to walk with a long stride knows it's fruitless... and funny. A child walking in Dad's shoes and wearing Dad's tie that hangs to their ankles is sweet and worthy of a quick picture. But I've also seen photos of unhoused people in the U.S. or children in small villages in Africa wearing clothes that are too big for them. These images tell a different story.

When it comes down to it, personality influences clothing choice the most. Many pop stars have become well-known based on what they choose to wear. Some people wear clothing to stand out, while others wear it to blend in. When my husband and I were dating, I had a favorite t-shirt I'd found at a thrift store. On it was a smiling hot dog in a bun pointing a thumb at himself. Next to the hot dog was the caption, "I love buns!" On a trip to visit my husband's parents, I didn't think twice about wearing that shirt out to lunch. But halfway through our meal my husband's father, a research scientist, asked me across the table his brow wrinkled in thought, "Is there a meaning to your shirt?"

The goofy theatre kid in me replied, "No. I just thought it was funny." I was expressing my personality through my clothing in a manner my father-in-law would never consider.

What clothes do your characters wear? If they picked out their favorite shirt, what would it look like? The personality of your characters will shine through their clothing choices. They'll set them up for the dream job they want to get or get them fired for wearing too short of a skirt to work. Their clothes will display their favorite cartoon character, the same one a hot potential love interest wears on their t-shirt during the meet-cute.

Lastly, consider color when deciding what your characters wear. My son is eight and loves to dress monochromatically. If his shirt is blue, his shorts should be too. It sets up some very silly combinations, but because that's his personality, we send him out the door anyway. In the play and movie *Steel Magnolias,* Shelby loves pink so much that her wedding is covered floor to ceiling in pink. And then there are those who are color blind like my husband. We've had many humorous moments when I've sent him back to our bedroom to pick out a new shirt to match his pants. He's also never forgiven me for making him get rid of a collared shirt he wore before we were married. In his mind the colors were beautiful. In my mind, they were atrocious. Seriously, that shirt was a blend of all the colors and patterns that were wrong with the 1990s.

The clothes people and characters choose to wear send messages to those around them. Some are clear while others are confusing. When writing your characters, think about the clothes they choose and how their choices are received by those around them.

A note on research

When researching clothing for characters, the process can be overwhelming. If looking for more modern styles, authors can look at clothing options offered online or advertised by influencers on social media. But when looking farther back in time, you have to be more creative. Some of my students in my costume design class have shared clothing research from the 1940s by showing me pictures of films or television shows from that time period. This is where I quickly stop them. Those pictures are of clothing chosen by a costume designer from that time. They aren't true to the clothing of that time. They are artistic choices made by someone, not the characters themselves.

If researching clothing from previous time periods, try to find photos that are of actual people. *Life* magazine was a fabulous resource from the past. It printed pictures of people simply living their lives. Other magazines and resources like this can also be found. And if you can't find these things, seek out sewing patterns. There was a time in the United States when families had to make their own clothes either because they lived rurally and far from stores or didn't have many financial resources. Patterns were widely used and are a great resource. If researching clothing from before the invention of the camera, look for paintings or other artwork of people from the era you're exploring.

My last note on research is that fabrics and clothing have changed in many ways with inventions. If you are writing a historical novel during the American Civil War and a man is slowly sliding off his lover's dress, be sure that he does not lower her zipper first. Zippers weren't invented until decades later. Also, consider modern fabrics such as polyester that only began being used in the mid-1900s.

Beware of stereotypes

When writing characters, I believe that all authors try to be true to the characters and create people (or animals, or fantastical beings) that are rich and honor who they are. That being said, I warn you to beware of stereotypes. For example, when I worked in the film industry as a professional extra I was booked to work on a film that took place at the Nebraska State Fair. I listened to the list of items the costume designers wanted us to bring and decided to have some fun. I dressed as country as I could. Overalls. A cotton, country flower-print shirt. I even put my hair in two braids. I did this as a joke. And can you guess what the costume designer said when I showed up for on-camera approval? "Perfect!" I dressed as a stereotype and they ate it up.

Sometimes, stereotypes can be useful in comedy. But beware of stereotypes if you are creating a character that you want your readers to take seriously.

Writing Rehearsal

Answer the questions below about your characters. If you are stuck and unsure, check out pictures, paintings, & patterns online.

- If your character has a job, what kind of clothing do they wear for their job?

- If your character was choosing their favorite shirt, what would it look like?

- If your character was choosing their favorite shoes, what would they look like?

- In which scenes in your WIP might your characters have to dress for a special occasion?

Chapter 7
THE ROVING THIRD HAND

Writing Fight and Romance Scenes Without Getting Your Characters Tangled

I'VE COVERED THE SIX elements of the drama as designated by Aristotle. But there are so many more elements of theatre we could cover. One area that I studied that Aristotle likely would never have thought of was stage combat and stunt work.

When I've shared this topic at workshops, I lovingly call this section "The Roving Third Hand." That comes from my husband's cousins. They're both jovial guys, well over six feet tall, and for a time owned a bar in Des Moines, Iowa. They enjoyed being playful with their patrons, especially when those patrons had overindulged. They had a trick they called "the roving third hand." If a couple was drunk and making out, one of the cousins would stand behind them and add his hand to one of the people's backs. He would rub his hand up and down with the person's back in unison with their lover's hands and wait for the person to realize there were three hands trailing down their back. Funny joke, right? Both the cousins got a kick out of it.

And, this is funny in this situation, but when reading a romance book with two lovers, finding three hands roving down a lover's back is more confusing than entertaining. The following tips and suggestions are to help you avoid a roving third hand in romance or fight scenes because an extra appendage in a fight scene will quickly rip your reader from the page with unanswerable questions.

I am a terrible singer. In college, when it came time to audition for musicals, I would be passable for the chorus but never good enough for a solo. But when it was time to learn stage combat, I shined. I loved working with a partner to tell a story using physical movements. Later as a grad student, I studied stage combat with the Society of American Fight Directors and was certified in five of their eight fighting styles using various weapons. After grad school, I attended the International Stunt School and learned how to perform precision driving, high falls, hand-to-hand combat, and more. I've performed professionally as a stunt performer and choreographed stage combat for the theatre. Creating realistic fights that are also safe for the actors is a challenge I love facing. The first time I was published in *Chicken Soup for the Soul* was for a story I wrote about being on a stunt team as one of the few women.

This is why there tends to be a fight somewhere in all my books. And this is also why I get frustrated reading poorly written combat scenes in books. I am not an expert on all types of fighting. I am nowhere near an expert on firearms. This section is focused on hand-to-hand combat, love scenes, and how to tell these stories in ways that your readers will be engrossed in the stories.

Fighting or loving, they're both a tangling of bodies. They come together. They pull apart. Sometimes there are more than two people involved. I have a dear friend who writes erotica and has told me things that leave me blushing for days.

Movement Phrases

How do we keep track of the people in space? A simple way is to sketch out the movements. These can be simple sketches showing hand and foot placements. In stage combat, I was taught to choreograph using "phrases." These phrases were sets of movements with beats, breaks, or transitions between them. A phrase could be as simple as a five-movement fight scene that ends with character A slapping character B on the backside with the blade of their sword. The phrase would be broken by character B jumping away and groaning in frustration. Then the fight would continue in the next phrase and so on until the end of the fight. When creating a love or fight scene, consider using these phrases. If you are sketching the movements, you could draw the hand and/or foot placements on your sketch indicating transitions or movements with arrows for one phrase. Start on a new page for another phrase and be sure to number them to keep them in order.

When sketching, you could also sketch like a coach for a football play. When I've directed plays, I've given a letter to each character in the play. On a copy of the set design, I write that letter and circle it to show where that character should be. Then I draw an arrow to their next position on the stage. I use multiple pages because if I didn't, my sketch would be a jumbled mess.

An example of tracking character movements is below. The set has three platforms in a U pattern, each with a single step to the floor. This scene is between character "A" and character "X." If the movements get busier, I sometimes add a number next to the character's indicator to show the movements step-by-step.

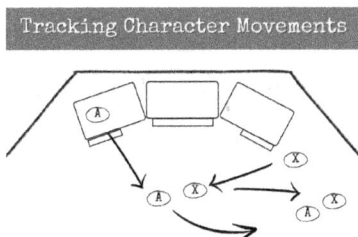

Tracking Character Movements

Writing Rehearsal

Create a sketch of the movements in a scene you've written or want to write. Write your first phrase, then try to add 2-4 more phrases to the fight or romantic entanglement.

- First, you will need a rough sketch of the setting. Indicate locations of furniture, important architecture (such as stairs), and other environmental elements (such as a large rock or a cliff's edge).

- Where on the set does each character start in the scene? Are they entering or already present?

- Identify areas where the characters come together and where they separate.

- Be specific with their movements. Someone shouldn't

just swing a sword at their opponent, they should thrust the sword at the opponent's upper arm trying to sever their deltoid muscle and make the opponent's arm useless. Someone shouldn't rub their lover's back, they should trace the ridges of muscles from shoulder to the the edge of their lover's waistband reveling in their lover's muscles tensing the further their hand roams.

Tracking Injuries

When writing fight scenes, another important element to keep track of is the injuries. In my debut novel, I realized as I wrote that I was causing a lot of damage to my characters. Some injuries were small but took a few days to heal. Others were much larger and affected the character's ability to move. To help track the injuries, I pulled up a template for a coroner's report. These reports have an outline of the human body on the front, and on the back is a space where the coroner can indicate injuries, scars, and other identifying marks. I printed copies for each of my characters and marked where injuries occurred as well as notes about the severity of the injury, how it affected the character's movement, how long it might take to heal, and any scars or marks left behind. If you search online for a coroner's report template, you'll find examples.

Keeping track of the injuries is important to me as a writer. This is because readers will be pulled out of the story if they read something they find unbelievable. I watched a campy action movie when I was in college in the 1990s. While I wasn't buying the whole storyline anyway, I actually got angry. This happened when one character nearly had their arm ripped off by an intergalactic insect and in the next scene was shooting a blaster roughly the size of a compact car. Maybe if they'd added a scene between these two scenes where one of the character's friends gave them a magical antidote I would have suspended my disbelief and accepted it. But they didn't. And it was just as ridiculous as the rest of the movie.

So, don't do this to your readers unless it's strategic and intentional. Yes, sometimes you're going to throw a plot twist that will infuriate your readers so much they throw the book across the room. (I hope to achieve this feat one day.) But if your goal isn't to pull your reader out of your story, keep track of those injuries and be sure that your characters display them too.

Movement Tracking in 3-D

So far, I've mentioned sketching out the characters' movements to keep track of them, but it can be a challenge to write a three-dimensional scene while tracking it in a two-dimensional manner. If you want to work in a three-dimensional way, my first trick is to find another person (or maybe more) to walk through the movements. Having been a stage director and fight choreographer, I have no qualms about asking people to move in certain patterns or hold positions. Of course, always do this in a manner that is safe and comfortable for everyone involved. Things could get awkward if you are choreographing a love scene and one of the people involved is the most modest and prudish person you know. (I've often been that person.)

In the film industry there are professional intimacy coordinators who work with the actors to ensure that all involved feel safe. Be this with your people. Or step into the scene yourself. On more than one occasion, I've asked my husband to step in as I worked through the intricacies of a fight scene. It's fun. We giggle. And he is again reminded that he married a creative person.

When doing this, your unsuspecting partner will feel most comfortable if you (1) ask about their comfort level before beginning, (2) move in slow motion, (3) explain or talk through each movement, and (4) only make light contact and only when absolutely necessary. If observing others as your models, follow these same guidelines and continually check in with your models on their comfort levels.

What happens though when you're writing last at night and there's no one to model for you? What do you do if anxiety keeps you from asking people to do this for you? What if something else is keeping you from having access to models?

Get creative. Use stuffed animals or Barbie dolls. If you're a parent like me, you might have some of these handy. For a scene I wrote in my debut novel, I totally wrote myself into a corner. I had eight characters hiking in a line down a path in the forest. A beast attacks from the front of the line, then another beast attacks from the back. As I started writing this scene I knew I was in trouble. I tried to find a way to edit the scene so I wouldn't have so many characters at this point. But I couldn't justify three of them either dropping dead or running away. After grumbling a few curse words, I came up with an idea and pulled out my kids' Lego bin.

I created eight Lego people to represent my characters. They were each unique and reflected my characters. Then I pulled out two tiny Minion figurines to represent the beasts. And this saved my scene. By using these silly toys, I was able to work step-by-step through what happens with each character in the scene. What's more important is that I was also able to write my scene in a way that the reader could follow all the action too.

Writing Rehearsal

What resources do you have to help you create a representation of your fight or romance scene in three dimensions?

- Dolls?

- Stuffed animals?

- Friends?

- Family?

- Something or someone else?

Make a list so you have it when you are ready when you need it.

The Physiological Effects of Violence

Now you've got plans for a scene and ways to keep track of your characters so they don't get tangled. Let's add another element to make it even more realistic. When I was studying stage combat, I once took a workshop on the physiological effects of violence. We explored what happens to the human body when violence is inflicted upon it. The instructor started with a slap to the face and worked his way up to disembowelment. I know, it's gross. But each step in the process showed us actors how to react appropriately to the stage violence we were portraying.

If you're punched in the nose, your eyes will water. This is why hitting an assailant in the nose is commonly a technique taught in self-defense. If the assailant can't see well because their eyes are watering, it gives the victim more opportunity to escape. In sword fighting, there was a technique where the combatants would try to slice their partner on the deltoid muscle (as I used for an example earlier). The deltoid is the muscle that bulges at the top of your arm and helps connect your arm and shoulder. They'd do this because if the deltoid is injured, that person can't use that arm well. It's the same reason some combatants aim for a knee. If the knee is injured, that person isn't going to be able to walk. Some of this is vulgar, I totally agree. But if you are writing fight scenes, it's important to acknowledge what you are doing to your characters and how it affects them.

What about the physiological effects of romantic touch and sensations? My husband once told me that at a certain international chain restaurant known for having orange shorts-clad sexy waitresses, these waitresses were trained to lightly trail their fingers over male patron's arms. Is this true? I honestly have no clue. But the theory behind it is brilliant. That light touch is intended to elicit a physiological effect. Gentle, romantic touch can cause an equal level of firing synapses and sensations as an aggressive, violent touch.

Certain areas of the body are more receptive to these touches and elicit different responses. Use your knowledge of these facts to write your character's reactions. Also, keep in mind that with romantic touch there might be some unique sensations characters prefer to elicit. For example, in college, I was in a play where I had to kiss a boy. Remember how I said I was a prude? I was then too. I hadn't kissed many boys and never in front of an audience. In a performance once, my acting partner bit my lip as he broke the kiss. In my mind, I thought it was just weird and hurt. Many years later when I told a friend about that lip bite, she said it sounded hot. With our characters, we need to know them well enough to know whether they think a certain touch is hot or weird or somewhere in between.

Writing Rehearsal

What physical responses could you include in your fight or romance scenes?

- Write a list.

- Use a thesaurus to help you create a varied list so you aren't accidentally stuck using the same descriptions.

- Specify a certain sensation that is particularly pleasurable or painful to your characters.

Vocalizations

Another reaction to violence is vocalization. When choreographing for the stage, we were taught to vocalize the fight scenes for two reasons. (1) To add to the believability of the fight and (2) to be sure we were still breathing. When some actors perform combat scenes, they are so focused they hold their breath and end the scene gasping for air. If someone screams in surprise or pain, the air goes out and more has to come in. This is where I like to introduce what I call "the belly button rule."

The rule is this: The closer an attack is to the belly button, the deeper the victim's voice will be in response. The further away from the belly button, the higher-pitched the vocal response will be. This is why a hit to the gut leaves a character grunting or groaning. But if some stomps on a character's toes, they'll often respond with a squeal. In film, the use of a Wilhelm scream is funny because of this rule. The Wilhelm scream is an odd, high-pitched scream sound effect used in many popular films. Often, it's used when a character is falling to their death. Something about it doesn't quite fit the gravity of impending death, therefore it is perceived as humorous. It can be found in many popular films. Search for it online and you'll surely find a video clip example of the Wilhelm scream. When you hear it, you'll know it.

When writing a physical scene, try to make the vocal sounds match the effect of touch. If they align perfectly, this will draw the reader into the scene more deeply and add to their rising heart rate. If the audible response doesn't match the physical stimulus, the reader will smirk or laugh at the oddity. Be intentional about your choices for the scene while being aware of your desired response from your reader.

Character Abilities

A final element to keeping fight and romantic scenes believable is knowing your characters' abilities. Being a middle-aged, slightly overweight woman, I've surprised a number of people when I've believably thrown a right hook or a left uppercut in a stage combat scene. Most people don't look at me and expect me to have this knowledge or skill.

What about your characters? Do they know how to fight? Or are they relying on their ability to avoid and run away? In a romantic scene, do the characters know how to map their partner's body to elicit the highest responses? Or are they prudish like me and giggle as they write that last sentence? Also, consider your characters' history and experiences that give them this knowledge or lack thereof.

Writing Rehearsal

You've already created character descriptions. Now add details about their abilities in combat and physical romance.

- Where are they knowledgeable?

- Where are they lacking in knowledge or ability?

- Identify this for each character that is involved in these kinds of scenes.

Take out the short scene you mapped out earlier in this chapter. Add specifics of the physical touch and the vocal responses.

- Is your scene a fight scene or a love scene?

- If it's a fight scene, who will win the fight in the end?

- If it's a romance scene, how does each character feel about the romantic touch and intimacy?

- Choose one particular touch and describe it in depth. How does each character respond to and feel about the touch?

Chapter 8
PUBLICITY & MARKETING

FOR THEATRE ARTISTS, LIKE authors, it's important to connect with an audience. If we didn't tell the community about our plays or musicals, they wouldn't come. If they were repeat customers, we asked them to join our mailing list so that we could connect with them and keep them posted on upcoming shows. We bought ads sometimes. We appeared on the morning news talking about our productions. If you want an audience, you must put your art out for the public to easily find.

Social Media

I will be quick to say that I don't like social media. But when it comes to publicity and marketing, even a small amount of social media interaction will help authors connect with readers. And I have found that I have been able to connect with other authors through social media. These authors have become friends, encouragers, and people I love meeting in real life. I recommend creating separate accounts, one for personal use and another for your author usage. If you use a penname, that's more easily done. In this world of technology, it's a good idea to control what information you put out widely to the world versus what's meant for close friends and family.

When it comes to social media, the benefits are that most communication can be done for free, and by posting regularly, you stay connected with readers and fellow authors. But there are so many choices these days, that you need to find the platform that works best for you. A big consideration when choosing social media platforms is where you'll find readers of your genre. Because my debut novel was a YA/teen novel, the marketing person with my publisher encouraged me to get on TikTok. I grumbled, but I did it because teens are active on TikTok. Find the platform where your readers are active. Join groups or chats. Basically, put yourself out there to your comfort level. Or don't. Some writers aren't on any social media and their books still sell quite well. But they do still market their books, just in other manners.

Do what works for you. If you are a new author, you might be searching for other authors. Check out groups on social media platforms where you can connect. I've found wonderfully amazing support through a few groups I've connected with on Twitter. (Yes, it has changed to X, but like many others, I still call it Twitter.) I never expected this when I joined, but I've met writers on Twitter who have inspired me, encouraged me, and empathized with me through my writing journeys.

Also, if you are querying, there are some great online events where you can put out your work. My debut novel was published by Parliament House Press. I was connected with them when I pitched my book in a Twitter pitch event, #DarkPit. An editor liked my pitch and asked for the full manuscript. These pitch events might come and go. Some like #PitMad and #PitchWars get so big they can't continue at their high volume and come to an end. Others pop up to replace them. So, whatever social media platform you're using, make friends, read the feeds when you can, and keep your eyes open for opportunities.

Writing Rehearsal

- Which social media platforms are you currently using? Are they for personal or professional use?

- Which social media platforms would be best for connecting with your readers?

- Which social media platforms would be best for connecting with other authors?

- If you aren't active on social media, choose one platform to start with and commit to making connections.

- If you aren't active on social media and don't intend to be, write out ideas for other methods of marketing your books.

Launch Team

So, you've written a book and it's being published. What can you do to get the word out? There are definitely ways to buy ads on social media sites or other areas. But word-of-mouth is also a great way to drum up interest in your book.

A common practice today is the launch team. These can be done in many different ways. Essentially, they include regular communication with a group of readers who agree to read your book and write reviews online just before your release.

When creating a launch team, I would recommend finding readers a minimum of one month before your release. Six to eight weeks is even better. This gives you time to assemble your team and get a copy of your book to them in time for them to read it before your release date.

Authors find launch team members in many ways: friends, family, social media, writing groups, etc. Wherever there are readers, you can find a launch team. You might want to limit the size of your team based on how you will run it. It's a common practice to have prize giveaways for participants. Readers are more likely to participate if they're given a free copy of your e-book and they have chances to win items. These prizes don't have to be huge. Many launch teams I've been on have given e-gift cards to popular places like Amazon or Starbucks. These are great because you don't have to pay to ship them. If you want to give out physical prizes, consider the cost and inconvenience of shipping the items. If you have unlimited time and money, then the sky's the limit. If you are watching your budget closely, you might consider smaller, flat items that can be easily dropped into an envelope.

The main objective of a launch team is to get people excited about your book and to have them post reviews. Keep that in focus as you communicate with your team. How you communicate depends on what you're comfortable with. Some authors use a private Facebook page, others use an email list. I was part of a launch team where the author had a Zoom party at the end. She drew names for prizes live on the video chat and answered questions about her book. Having a handful of book reviews posted online before your release will build interest from readers. Reviews help spread the news of your book by word of mouth.

There are other sites where you can release your book for early reviews but some will require a fee. NetGalley is a popular site for readers to find ARCs (Advanced Reading Copies). There are incentives for readers to post timely reviews that will appear before your release. Because the internet is constantly changing, I recommend that you connect with other authors to find the websites that have worked best for them as you are getting closer to your release date.

Writing Rehearsal

- Where could you find people to be on your launch team? Make a list of people you know who might be interested.

- What is the timeline for your book release? Write out specific dates.

- If you plan to give out prizes, what kinds of prizes are you able to give out with your current budget?

∿

Launch Party

Another idea to connect with local readers is to arrange a launch party. Like a launch team, this can be as simple or as complicated as you want it to be. If you are keeping it simple, host a small party with cookies and lemonade in your backyard or at a local park. Invite people to come for treats and to purchase a signed copy of your newly released book.

At a conference I attended, an author shared the idea of business partnerships to help boost your launch party. When I had a launch party for my debut novel, I contacted the owner of a local coffee shop and asked if I could have it at her place. She was very supportive of the arts and local artists and quickly checked her calendar for a time that worked for both of us.

Here I'll encourage you to be bold and put yourself out there. While emailing the coffee shop owner, I thought it couldn't hurt to ask if she'd like to donate a gift card I could use in a giveaway. I was nervous, afraid I was asking for too much. To my surprise, she gave me three gift cards! I can't promise it will always work out for you so well, but I will encourage you to kindly ask for things like this. I continued asking friends with local businesses. By the time I was done gathering donations for my debut novel launch party, I had ten prize packs to give away that included gift cards, coffee mugs, pens, locally made lip balm, and two dozen eggs from a farmer. I assembled the various gifts and included a business card from all the donors in each gift bag for help promote them.

Another giveaway I organized for my launch party were a limited number of book-themed simple items. I created bookmarks with recipes from my book, a map of the island in my book, and single tea packets. When I advertised my launch party, I was able to guarantee the first 20 people who bought a book would get a free book-themed gift and everyone attending would be entered into the giveaways.

Writing Rehearsal

Make another list.

- What connections do you have with local businesses? Start simple. What about your insurance agent? They often have promotional pens.

- Make a list of local businesses you might not have a connection with and are willing to approach. I continue to encourage connecting with local businesses because I encourage support of local businesses. Also, they tend to be more willing and quick to offer promotional items than corporations.

- Now, make a list of possible locations for your launch party. A local business? A library? A church? A community center?

Book Signings & Author Visits

Another part of publicity is connecting with readers through bookstores and libraries. Visit a local independent bookstore and ask if you can host a book signing. Be sure to do this months in advance as some fill their schedules quickly. I've had a great time signing at bookstores. I get to meet readers and talk about my book and do so in a place where people love books. It helps if you set up a display table with your book, promotional materials, and giveaway items.

Promotional materials could be as simple as a bookmark or business card with your contact information. Giveaway materials could be candies or something that's significant to your book. When signing books for my debut novel, I always give out packets of herbal teas because they directly tie to my book. Book signings are also a great way to collect contact information from readers for your newsletter lists. If they are writing out their information on a paper, be sure that you confirm you can read their handwriting. Or you could have a tablet or laptop for people to sign up electronically or print a QR code that links to a Google form to collect the email address. Sometimes, I have offered a giveaway of an e-gift card for anyone who signs up to garner more participation.

When approaching libraries, keep in mind that they have tight schedules too. But having worked at a library, I can tell you that they often have summer programs where they are looking for inexpensive presenters. At our library, the rule was that if an author presented a program for free, they could sell their books at the end of the signing. When reaching out to libraries, it's helpful to ask about policies like this in advance.

It might be overwhelming to think about presenting a program at a library. Start simple. If you write for children, you could read from your book or books and ask the children questions after you read. Because children love visual and tactile stimulation, having stuffed animals or toys that match the theme of your book helps. Also, consider printing out copies of coloring sheets that also go with your theme. Many free coloring sheets can be found online.

When working with teens or adults, a book reading is also often welcome. But with these groups, they are also interested in the craft and/or business of writing. Think about the basic elements necessary to write a book, design the cover, and market the book. Think back to your early days of writing and the questions you had about writing a book and getting it published. Share your experiences and maybe you'll inspire another great author.

Libraries and local businesses are great places to connect with readers and share your writing. Use connections you've already established in your community to set up these events. And if you don't have these connections, be bold and brave. Put yourself out there and see where it leads you.

Writing Rehearsal

- Do you want to organize a book signing at a local bookstore? Make a list of the bookstores you could approach.

- Would you like to present a program at a library? Make a list of libraries in your area. If there are multiple branches, ask if you can visit more than one of them.

Book Festivals & Conferences

To book festival or to not book festival? That is the question. I write this as I sit at a large book festival with over 150 authors. I've been on a panel for a workshop sharing techniques for writing fight scenes. And I've sat at my book table amongst a sea of other authors at book tables for a day and a half.

I still haven't decided if it was worth the time and effort to come to this festival or not. I've only sold one book. One. Book. That's all. And only five people attended the panel I spoke on. But, I have given away multiple bookmarks and promotional materials. I've also set up a giveaway for a gift card where I am collecting email addresses for my mailing list.

Going to book festivals can be a great way to connect with readers. It's up to each author to decide whether or not it's worth the time and effort to attend. At this festival, I will not make money, I'll lose it in fact. Yes, I've connected with readers, and yet I don't know if I'd come to this particular event again.

On the other hand, I've attended an author festival in a town not far from my home. In this town, I have some connections and know other authors. I sold many more books there and still made connections with readers.

The benefit of book festivals is not only connecting with readers, but also connecting with authors. There's more on building community in the next chapter. But the best part of connecting with authors at a festival is seeing how others do their marketing and book tables. I've gotten lots of ideas about the best kinds of swag and table layouts by watching others. When I go to a conference with vendors or authors, I like looking at what items I might want and use. Yes, it's fun to have free candy, but if everyone else is giving out candy, how can that make your book table stand out?

When offering a giveaway, there are many kinds of prizes that readers enjoy. I often give away an e-gift card because it's easy to email later to the winner. An author friend gave away a book-themed basket filled with treats connected to her novel. There are a plethora of ideas for giveaways. Sometimes authors will work together to create a book basket, each contributing one of their books. These can be popular because prize winners get a bigger prize, so more will enter. Using the theme of the book, authors can create a giveaway where the winner will receive a copy of the author's book and a donation to a charitable organization that is reflective of the theme, characters, or location of the book.

The sky is the limit when it comes to giveaways. The most important thing to do is try something and see if it works for you or not. If not, try something different. Consider your readers and what they might like to win. Consider different ways to connect with them in person or online through social media. Again, the sky's the limit.

Writing Rehearsal

- Are there book festivals in your area? Check out local libraries and literary groups. Make a list.

- What kind of swag or giveaway items could you give out at a book table? Consider the simplest and least expensive (yes, this could be candies) up to something that might take more investment (notebooks, pens, or other items with your logo or contact info).

- If you were to give away a special item or prize, what could it be? What would your target readers enjoy? Can you choose something that connects with your book?

Newsletters

So far, I've shared ways to connect with readers for first contact. But once you connect with them, it's great to continue to build that relationship. In today's world, this can be done via a digital newsletter. At each book signing, launch party, or library visit, ask readers if they'd like to sign up for your newsletter. As I mentioned before, I've offered prizes to those on my newsletter list. By planning a giveaway a week after an event, you might get more people to sign up.

Digital newsletters can be created on multiple platforms and often for free. When starting your writing career, use all the free resources you can. There are other books out there that give specific guidance on best practices for sending newsletters. My basic rules are: (1) Keep it short and simple, (2) Don't pester your readers, and (3) Send the newsletter at a time when people are commonly at their computers.

Keep it short and simple. My favorite newsletters are ones that are easy to skim and quick to read. Using large-font headers and/or separating sections with colors or lines helps people skim through your newsletter quickly to see the basics of the content and decide where they'd like to read further.

Don't pester your readers. The quickest way to lose a newsletter subscriber is to blow up the reader's inbox. There are times when writers are releasing books and they feel like there is a lot to share, so they send daily updates. Other times, writers are writing or editing and don't have many updates. Avoid sending newsletters feast or famine-style. Instead, stay consistent. What works for me is to have a regular reminder in my phone and on my calendar to send a newsletter every two weeks. Not only does this remind me to send newsletters, but it also reminds me not to send them.

Send the newsletter at a time when people are commonly at their computers. Newsletters sent on Friday evenings will likely get lost in a string of emails received over the weekend. Instead, choose a time when readers are more likely to be online to send the newsletter. When is this? Honestly, it's often when people are at work. In my limited experience, I've found that more of my newsletters are opened by readers when they're sent on Tuesdays mid=morning. This is after the inbox has been cleared on Mondays and before everything piles up throughout the week.

Writing Rehearsal

Create your newsletter plan.

- Which platform would you use? Mailchimp? MailerLite? Other?

- How might you design the newsletter to be eye-catching? Consider branding, colors, and layout.

- How frequently do you plan to send a newsletter? What time specifically would you send the newsletter to grab the most attention?

Mailings

Mailings sent through the post office can still be effective. But I would suggest targeting specific people or groups if you send them. For example, my debut novel featured a main character who had become hard of hearing after an illness. Having had connections with the Deaf community, I targeted Deaf schools across the country. I sent a postcard to the high school librarian that emphasized that the book featured characters with disabilities.

Consider ways in which your book could connect with a specific audience such as a geographical area, a business or nonprofit, a sports group, or an organization that reaches various professionals such as the American Dental Association or the Women in Dairy group.

Writing Rehearsal

- Create a list of people, groups, or organizations you could target for a mailing campaign.

- What would you send to them to target these people, groups, or organizations? Postcard? Email? Complimentary copy of your book? Others?

Creating a Marketing Budget

When planning for marketing for your book and its release, all authors should set a budget for what they are willing to contribute financially. Take a moment to do that. How much can you afford to spend on promotional materials, travel to signings, free copies of your book, etc.? You may not have a concrete idea to start with, and that's okay. But start with some kind of budget or you might find your writing becoming more of a hobby that you spend money on instead of a business where you profit financially.

Chapter 9
BUILDING YOUR TRIBE AND THICKENING YOUR SKIN

Building Your Tribe

WHILE WRITING CAN BE a lonely adventure, it doesn't have to be. And in my opinion, it shouldn't be. Building a community of authors and other creatives will help you as you journey through the waters of writing and publishing.

How do you build your tribe? I always recommend finding a local writers' group. These are great places to share writing, ideas, and tips. I've made many friends through my local writing group. Very few of them write in my genre. But they have years of experience and suggestions on marketing and publishing. One friend, Larry, is a retired teacher who self-publishes his books. If I ever have questions about self-publishing, Larry is the first person I email. Some authors will be reluctant to share ideas and tips like this because they are worried about competition. The publishing world is a difficult one, and many people are fighting with everything they have to get their books into readers' hands. Some authors choose to keep their successes close to their hearts. Not Larry. Because we write in very different genres, we know that our books will not compete and he is happy to share tricks of the trade.

The benefit of a local writing group is that you'll meet a variety of people with a variety of experiences who want to share ideas and help each other succeed. At least, this has been my experience. After you've been writing for a while and had your own experiences, you might find yourself leading a workshop or sharing ideas with newer writers just starting to dip their toes into the waters.

It's also wonderful to connect with authors in your genre. They are the ones who are more knowledgeable of the genre and the trends within the genre. You might find fellow authors like this in a local writing group, and you might not. There are many ways to connect with other authors including through social media. As mentioned previously, social media can be used to connect with readers and writers. On Twitter, I've found many authors who not only write in my genre but also have similar life experiences as myself. One group I've connected with is a group of writers who are also moms. Every life experience has its challenges. I've enjoyed sharing the challenges of parenting and writing with this group. My first novel, I jokingly called a "naptime novel." That's not because it's a great read to help you go to sleep. It's because I only worked on it while my kids were napping. I've loved finding support from this group of mom writers who get it and get me in a way others don't.

Another benefit of connecting with writers in your genre is finding critique partners. I love my beta readers, friends who read my books and support my writing. Some of them are too nice and won't critique my book in deeper ways. Finding a critique partner who knows my genre and isn't a close friend means they have no problem providing deeper criticism.

Connecting with writers online can be helpful if you live in an area without many writing groups. As I write this, I'm looking out the window at the tree-lined street with neighbors walking as the summer sun begins to dip toward the horizon. This town is quaint with less than 10,000 residents. It's also at least a 45-minute drive to my "local" writing group. I love visiting Larry and the others in my group, but sometimes I can't go because of the logistics of the commute. But I can easily pull out my phone and participate in a live chat for writers on social media. Or, if you're in a small town like me, consider starting your own writer's group. With my connections to the local library, I've discussed this with the program director a few times.

By attending writing conferences, authors can connect with each other too. This can be done by sharing business cards and following each other on social media. But it's more fun to build a deeper community when you can. I was fortunate to meet a group of women at a conference that we all just clicked. We write across genres from picture books to thrillers to erotica and many genres in between. We shared stories and laughed our way through the conference. When one of the authors suggested we start a Facebook group, we all jumped on it. Over the past few years, a few new authors have joined us. There we share our journeys in writing. Sometimes we celebrate our successes with a new book release or a trip to a festival. Other times, we share the challenges of rejections and life events that keep us from writing. I love this group and wish that every author could find people like this that keep me laughing my way through writing and helping lift me up when I'm down.

Lastly, I'll say that building your tribe can take time. Some friends will come and go. There are people I enjoyed meeting early in my writing journey who have slipped away and I've lost contact with. In those voids, new authors have come along to share in the adventures of writing. Enjoy the tribe you have when you have them and stay open to finding new writing friends along the way.

Writing Rehearsal

- Who is in your tribe? Which friends do you have as beta readers? Will they critique lightly or deeply? Make a list.

- Are you part of a writing group? If so, are there others you'd like to join? Make a list.

- If you are not part of a writing group, seek one out. Is there one locally that you could visit?

- Where can you connect with other authors online? Have you found authors in your genre? Seek out groups online that you can connect with. Where will you find them?

The Rejection Section

I have yet to meet someone who loves being rejected. So, curl up with a soothing beverage, and let's talk about the most painful part of writing, the evil R word: rejection.

When working as an actor or studying in college and grad school, I was rejected often. I didn't get cast or didn't get cast in the role I really, really wanted. It hurt. Every. Single. Time. It took me a while to see beyond the casting process and to discover that often I wasn't cast because of something out of my control. And, this is very true for publishing too.

For example, during my last year of grad school, auditions were held for the three main stage shows. I put all my hope in being cast in Shakespeare's *A Winter's Tale*. I had wanted to perform the beautiful, lyric lines penned by the Bard. Because I'm writing this here, you'll probably guess I didn't get cast in that show. I was cast, but in a different play, *Anton in Showbusiness*. This show was a statement play. It was making a statement about how there are twice as many women acting in theatre and half as many roles. So, all roles in the play were performed by women. I ended up playing a Texas businessman, a Romanian director, and an English director.

At first, my feelings were hurt, but I accepted the role and got to work. A few weeks into rehearsals, I was talking to the play's director as we ate lunch. She was a fellow grad student studying directing and this show was her big thesis project. "Annie, no one else could perform this role. I told the other directors they couldn't have you," she told me. I was initially surprised, but she continued explaining that I was the best person to perform the different dialects and could create these odd characters. What was heartbreak at not being cast in a Shakespearian play turned into one of the best compliments I was ever given as an actor. Sometimes, rejection for one thing can lead to a much better opportunity.

Heartbreak happens. Often I've heard people tell others to "just get over it" or "shake it off." That works for some, but not everyone. I find it helpful to acknowledge the hurt, the pain. In a way, greet the emotion, recognize it, then allow myself to let it go. Invite it to stay for dinner, but don't let it move into the basement where it'll live for years.

Sadly, it's often true that the more rejection one faces, the tougher their skin becomes. The hurt hurts a little less each time. If you don't believe this, go on Twitter. There are so many posts from authors describing the journey they've taken to publication. One of my Twitter writer friends recently published a book seven years after first querying it. It hurt to be rejected again and again, but she used those rejections as motivation to spur her forward. She revised. She asked beta readers to read it again. And then she revised some more. Now, she's enjoying some well-deserved success on the publication of her book.

A warning here though: If you are in the throws of rejection and it hurts to see all these success stories, give yourself a break from reading or hearing them. I believe it's perfectly fine to step away, take a breath, and settle your heart before going back online.

There are many stories of how authors deal with rejections. When rejections used to come as a letter in the mail, authors might collect them to ceremoniously burn once they got their first big publishing deal. The first rejection I got from a big agent who'd requested my full manuscript was an email, but I printed it out and kept it on my desk for months as I continued to query. That visual reminder helped push me to keep going.

Another visual reminder I used was collecting beads as I queried. These are jewelry beads I'd bought at the craft store years ago when I used to make beaded jewelry. I picked out a nice clear jar and put it in my office. Every time I sent my manuscript out to an agent or editor, I put a bead in the jar. If I got a full manuscript request, I added a special bead, sometimes with special meaning to the full request. Once my debut novel was published, I strung the beads into a necklace. I still wear that necklace to book signings and author events.

As I added beads to my jar, I realized I could look at each bead in one of two ways. I could see them as reminders of my failures, or I could see them as a reminder of the times I believed in my work so strongly that I put it out into the world. I chose the second option. By using these beads, I could visually see a representation of my faith in my work. And I'm proud to wear my necklace to remind me of all the work I put into getting my book into readers' hands.

Rejection hurts. But it's also part of being an artist and putting your art into the world. As an actor, I had much practice being rejected. I feel that this gave me an edge when I first started querying. When you are going through the process of seeking an agent, an editor, or even finding readers, stay strong. Don't let one bad review or rejection ever make you question your writing. Believe in yourself and surround yourself with a support team to cheer you on. And if all else fails, I hear rage rooms are great for burning off those feelings of anger and frustration.

Writing Rehearsal

Consider how you plan to handle rejection.

- Describe how it feels to be rejected or to have a bad review of your work. How can you adjust your perspective of the rejection to ease the hurt?

- I collected beads in a jar to help me deal with rejection. Make a plan for a way in which you can deal with rejection.

- If you are part of a writing group, consider how you can encourage your writing partners when they face rejection.

Defining Success

What does success mean to you as an author? Is it simply writing one book from start to finish? Is it being a multiple *New York*

Times best-selling author? Is it just writing something that will make a reader feel something?

When dealing with rejection, I feel it's important to define success for yourself so you're reminded of what you're striving for as you face roadblocks. Success can be defined in so many ways. An area where authors have difficulty with their progress is when they set very high goals and have their hearts broken when they don't reach them quickly. When I lived in Los Angeles, I was talking to my friend, Alaina, over lunch one day. We were making plans to get together to watch a movie. When I offered the next evening, she said she couldn't because she was planning to attend a going away party for her friend, someone I didn't know. I asked why the friend was leaving town, and Alaina shrugged saying dryly, "She's a singer and she discovered that they don't give you Grammy awards when you walk off the plane." This singer-friend had set her goals so high she couldn't be successful within the parameters she'd set.

In the world of acting, it's often said that there are no overnight successes. Yes, an actor might appear to burst on the scene and skyrocket to stardom. Usually, that burst is a slow burn of years of training, auditioning, rejection, and repeating all this over and over again. As authors, I encourage you to reach for the sky. Do you want to be a household name like Stephen King? Do you want to write books with the rapidity of James Patterson? If yes, then I'm cheering you on from the sidelines.

When considering your goals, I recommend a multistep process. Yes, aim high, but choose those smaller goals you must accomplish to get there. In education, there is often discussion of SMART goals, goals that are: Specific, Measurable, Attainable, Realistic, and Time-bound. When making writing goals, choose SMART goals. An example of a smart goal in writing could be: I will write a 70,000-word historical romance set during the Regency era and complete my first draft within six months. If this timeframe works with your lifestyle, this would be a SMART goal.

So, use those SMART goals to build or scaffold your way to your ultimate goal. After writing the book, maybe it goes to beta readers or an editor. Set a timeline for your book. If you are self-publishing, set a time for the book cover design to be complete and choose a release date. I don't know about you, but with my scattered mind, I find that I must make time-bound goals or I'll never get a book done. That's why I'm typing this furiously while my husband has my kids at an event. My goal is to finish work on this section of the book by tomorrow.

Let's stop for a second and talk about grace. When setting goals, there might be times that you don't reach them. What do you do then? Give yourself the grace you need and/or the kick-in-the-pants motivation you need. Talk to your tribe. But don't beat yourself up. Acknowledge you didn't reach a goal, decide how to do better with completing it and how you'll handle the next goal, then get back to work. Don't wallow in the frustration and disappointment, recognize that you are a human being who will make mistakes... but you'll also make it right.

Writing Rehearsal

Set some goals now for a current WIP or upcoming project.

- What is your ultimate goal for this novel?

- Define one goal you could complete in the next two weeks to move your project toward the ultimate goal.

- Write three (or more) SMART goals to complete that would lead you toward your ultimate goal.

Yourself, the person vs. yourself, the artist

I've seen some artists, actors & writers, who are trying so hard to please others that they lose themselves in the process. This is extremely easy to do on social media. Artists live under pressure to perform or produce and it can be overwhelming. It's tempting to follow a trend or represent ourselves as something different or more perfect than we are. And it doesn't help that so many influencers on social media are constantly showing off their "perfect" lives.

Many artists create a public persona. For example, Annie Lisenby isn't my true name. It's my pen name, my public persona. I use it to separate Annie, the teacher and mom, from Annie, the writer of romance and occasionally vampires. For me, this was important because of my teaching job and some positions I hold in my small town. I know that there are people in some of my social groups who don't approve of what I write. There aren't many of them, but they are there. And truly, that's okay. I'm not here to make everyone happy. But by having a pen name, I can hide behind the mask of Annie Lisenby when I'm doing writer things and take off that mask when I'm at a meet and greet for a community organization.

As artists, we need to know who we are as a person and who we are as an artist. Often, those characteristics will overlap. For example, when I was working as a professional film and television extra, I was approached by an extras casting director that represented a cable television show that was known for showing a lot of nudity. Other extras nudged me saying, "You know if you go topless, you'll make more money." What they didn't know was that I had defined my acting boundaries before I moved to Los Angeles. And nudity was not something I was willing to do. I still got other work, and I was much more comfortable on set and proud of myself. In this example, who I was as a person was aligned with who I was as an artist.

What's important to consider here is whether or not you know who you are and who you want to portray as an author. In the comedy movie *Tropic Thunder,* the character Kirk Lazarus played by Robert Downey, Jr. plays an actor in a movie known for working very deeply on his characters. When challenged about this, Lazarus replies, "I know who I am. I'm the dude playin' the dude, disguised as another dude!" I love this quote because it so truly captures the confusion some artists have when trying to separate who they are as a person from who they are as an artist.

Instead of holding on to Lazarus' words, hold on to the Bards. "To thine own self be true." No matter what kind of writer you are, be true to yourself, know yourself, and know how much of yourself you want to share publicly.

Writing Rehearsal

Consider who you are and who you are as an author.

- Do you use a pen name? Why or why not?

- What do you want readers to know about you?

- What are elements about yourself that you would not want to share online? Consider things such as your family (especially photos of kids), what state you live in, or other details about yourself.

ACKNOWLEDGEMENTS

To my readers, thank you. Without you, the art of writing is incomplete. Thank you for spending your precious time with my words.

I have to thank all my writer friends in the Good-Selling Authors Club. Your support as I started leading workshops and for your pushes for me to write this book are what got me to these final pages.

To all my other writer friends I know IRL and only online, thank you for your kindness and sharing this writing adventure with me.

Thank you to Agent Amy for your honest and clear direction on my writing adventures. You always shoot me straight, and I love that about you.

To my book club, thank you for being my earliest beta readers. We've all moved or taken new jobs and rarely see each other, but your early support helped give me the confidence I needed to make it to this point.

To my children, thank you for the times you let me write, even if dinner was late sometimes.

To my husband, your support means the world to me. Thank you for occasionally sending me on writing retreats and saying "yes" to so many ideas I've had when writing.

To all the people I've shared the stage, the screen, or the classroom with, you are the reason for this book. Your pursuit of art is admirable and created a safe place for me and others to grow in our art.

annie

About the Author

Annie Lisenby is a native of the Missouri Ozarks. She has BA and MFA degrees in Theatre and teaches theatre at a rural college. During her younger years, she worked as a stage actress, stunt performer, and background actor for film and television. Annie's debut novel *A Three-Letter Name* was selected as the best indie published book by an author from Missouri for 2022 through the Indie Author Project.

When not teaching and writing, Annie is involved in several community groups and loves exploring the Ozark hills with her husband and two children.

She loves to connect with readers through her newsletter and on social media. Connect with her and find out more about Annie and her writing at www.annielisenby.com.

Annie is available for speaking engagements and workshops.